Map OF NEW-ORLEANS AND ENVIRONS

Engraved expressly for Cohen's Directory

BY J.T.HAMMOND.

1850.

THE PLANTATION COOKBOOK

THE PLANTATION COOKBOOK

THE JUNIOR LEAGUE OF NEW ORLEANS

ILLUSTRATED BY M. DELL WELLER

B. E. TRICE PUBLISHING, INC., NEW ORLEANS, LOUISIANA

The purpose of the Junior League is exclusively educational and charitable and is to promote voluntarism; to develop the potential of its members for voluntary participation in community affairs; and to demonstrate the effectiveness of trained volunteers.

ISBN 0-9631925-0-7
(previously published by Doubleday, ISBN 0-385-01157-1)
Library of Congress Catalog Card Number 72-84921

DEDICATION

The profit realized by the Junior League of New Orleans, Inc., from the sale of *The Plantation Cookbook* will be used for projects which we sponsor for the betterment of the community, and it is to these endeavors we dedicate our book.

ACKNOWLEDGMENTS

The Junior League of New Orleans, Inc., expresses gratitude to the active and sustaining members and their many Louisiana friends who gave unselfishly of their time and talents to help with the publishing of this book. We also wish to acknowledge the following: Mrs. Connie G. Griffith and William Cullison, Special Collections Division, Howard-Tilton Memorial Library, Tulane University; Collin B. Hamer and Staff, Louisiana Division, New Orleans, The New Orleans Public Library; Theo H. Harvey, Jr.; Mrs. Inez V. Hebert, Administrator, The Shadows-on-the-Teche; Leonard V. Huber; Mrs. Henry F. Means; and Department of Archives and Louisiana Room, Louisiana State University Library.

CONTENTS

ILLUSTRATIONS

NEW ORLEANS

NEW ORLEANS, the Crescent City, is today a romantic, gracious, ever-inviting place to live and visit—particularly in the springtime. The beauty of its homes and gardens, plus the enchantment of its past, annually lure visitors to the area. Southern hospitality opens many doors including those to some of New Orleans' loveliest homes. By touring these houses, guests in the city can begin to understand the culture and heritage which is obviously, even passionately, kept alive by native New Orleanians.

As a major American city, New Orleans is greatly dependent of the prosperity and continuing expansion of its port. Rated second only to that of New York in terms of value of foreign commerce and tonnage of water-borne cargo, the port of New Orleans does an annual business involving three billion dollars. In fact, the location of the city—its placement on the Mississippi River—has always been the one most important factor in its history.

In 1718, Jean Baptiste Le Moyne Sieur de Bienville, a Canadian explorer, founded New Orleans. He chose a site ninety miles above the mouth of the Mississippi, intending it as a garrison of sorts. Bienville was convinced that it was from this river vantage point that the vast French territory in Louisiana could best be controlled. The city developed into a gateway metropolis of international importance very quickly and from extremely humble beginnings.

The site picked was actually one long used by Indians on their way from the Mississippi to a ridge running along a picturesque waterway that settlers called Bayou St. John. The Bayou is open to Lake Pontchartrain, and because of its adjacent high ground was actually—though sparsely—settled even before New Orleans. This Bayou area gradually became a popular Creole suburb which grew in grandeur during the brief period of Spanish dominion (1764–1800) in the Louisiana territory.

New Orleans itself was established in a canebrake, and early residents grew quite accustomed to picking their way along unpaved streets that were sometimes under water from rain or flood. Drainage ditches were dug and levees, or dikes, built in an effort to ward off Mississippi River floodwaters. Uniform streets and city squares were laid out in a rectangular pattern and bounded by the river, Rampart Street, Canal Street, and Esplanade Avenue. Settlers protecting their city from marauders built a moat and wooden palisade on three sides. Gates were provided for carriage traffic at three points—two near the river, on Canal Street and on Esplanade Avenue, and the last at Rampart and Governor Nichols Street. No doubt the Rampart Street gate handled the most traffic as it was regularly used by residents of Bayou St. John.

Plantations up and down the fertile Mississippi shores prospered and New Orleans became a rare urban jewel in this lush, but rural, setting. The lifeblood of the old city, or Vieux Carré, was the river and the large volume of trade it brought. As Louisiana planters accumulated wealth, so did residents of the city. Soon a delightful society flourished and grew until the social advantages of New Orleans surpassed the big cities of America and, at least in local exclusiveness, rivaled the courts of Europe.

The Duc d'Orléans, the future king of France, and his two brothers, great-great grandsons of the regent of France for whom the city was named, received a warm welcome when they visited the colony in the late eighteenth century. Fashionable Creoles eagerly entertained the royal guests—and their cooks turned out splendid dinners in their honor. Creole menus could be very elaborate, have five to six courses, and on occasion were enriched by imported continental delicacies such as anchovies and brandied fruits. Creoles also imported, and drank, enormous quantities of wines which they bought in barrels at auction. Gentlemen settled their differences on the field of honor; gambling was a social institution and dancing a Creole passion. Colorful operas, plays, and public balls were regularly attended during winter months. Times were gay; chivalry was in full bloom.

Creole New Orleans boasted an elite and very social "winter season" which now coincides with Carnival, the period from Epiphany to Ash Wednesday. Planters and their families arrived annually in the city after the harvesting of crops, and just in time for the opening of the opera. They brought along the necessary number of slaves to insure domestic comfort during their winter residence in New Orleans. If they were very rich, these families usually owned a town house. The rural planters enjoyed the city's social activities, and at the same time they handled business transactions in New Orleans pertaining to the running of a successful plantation.

Floods, hurricanes, and epidemics of yellow fever failed to daunt social and physical growth of the city. Even two disastrous fires only inspired the plucky French and Spanish residents to rebuild bigger and better homes and commercial buildings.

Vieux Carré houses were built only a step or two from the banquette (sidewalk) and, because space was precious, were crowded close together, often sharing a common wall. Early builders, using soft Louisiana bricks in construction, learned to protect walls from the damp by finishing them with coats of plaster. The tropical climate encouraged the custom of having parterres (gardens). Visitors still marvel at the lovely plants, herbs, and trees that manage to flourish in these small enclosed patios.

In the early nineteenth century, daily commercial activities centered in areas around the levee and the river-front French Market. Sailors and laborers of different nationalities, merchants, planters, and their agents, all visited the levee and used the wide thoroughfare atop it. The New Orleans river front was alive with people and ships, and an ever increasing number of foreign and domestic vessels regularly plied the river.

Creole families considered mealtimes the focal point of any day and meals evolved into long, elaborate affairs. In prewar days, Negro slaves shopped daily for their owners buying the meats, seafoods, vegetables, and spices required for Creole dishes. The French Market, which is still a beehive of activity, was at first the only central market place. Trading was brisk and from early morning hours a babble of voices in many different tongues and dialects grew to a crescendo of noise which gradually diminished when the place closed at noontime. Negro women balancing broad baskets on their heads hawked hot delicacies and garden dainties along with items from the market's open stalls. These *marchandes* (street vendors) walked the Vieux Carré, loudly chanting their wares, providing a convenience to Creole housewives while hopefully bringing a small profit to the marchande herself.

Retail shops sprang up along Chartres and later Canal Street. Madame Olympé offered the finest in French chapeaux while Madame Pluché displayed fashionable gowns. All could be purchased on premises or sent by messenger for "Madame" to make her selections at home. Creole ladies eventually relaxed their confining, shy ways, and began to visit Vieux Carré shops. Only in one respect were the Creoles steadfastedly stubborn and this was in accepting "foreigners" into their exclusive society.

The barrier was particularly felt by the Americans who had come from other areas of the country in great numbers after the Louisiana Purchase in 1803. These aggressive newcomers did not understand or accept the Creole way of life or the French language. Their Puritan heritage and somber ways did not prepare them for the Creole's love of luxury and frivolity. Americans had never taken siestas; they wanted no part of gambling or dueling. They were not addicted to dancing and were bewildered by the Creole habit of walking through muddy streets in court dress to go to balls. Finally, they emphatically disapproved of the Catholic Creole's festive celebration of the Sabbath.

The Americans established new neighborhoods, businesses and social activities of their own and continued to speak English. They had come to Louisiana to make money—and many did—allowing a heated competition to develop between Creole and American residents. Success and wealth were displayed through social functions set in impressive surroundings. Consequently, in the nineteenth century, American and Creole architecture became more and more grandiose.

The protection afforded by early palisades and moat was no longer required in the bustling city. New Orleans was no longer confined to the Vieux Carré. Down-river of the old city on the other side of Esplanade Avenue, Bernard Marigny developed his family plantation into a Creole suburb— appropriately named Faubourg Marigny. Unfortunately, the grand dreams of this inexperienced developer were never fully realized and only on Esplanade itself were a few fashionable French homes ever built.

The Americans, however, were more fortunate since experienced promoters developed their suburbs. The first, Faubourg St. Mary, was on the upriver side of Canal Street reaching eventually as far as Felicity Street. Not only was a fashionable residential neighborhood built here, but also a soaring commercial one, which by the 1840s and '50s was perhaps one of the richest single sections in the country. Today, warehouses have taken over the old buildings. Only an experienced eye can discern the once elegant "thirteen buildings" on Julia Street—between Camp and St. Charles Streets—that housed some of the most prominent American families living in New Orleans during the middle of the nineteenth century.

As commerce expanded in Faubourg St. Mary, the Americans looked further upriver for new and larger areas in which to build their homes. Enterprising promoters began buying nearby plantations to divide and sell them off in large lots. Finally American architecture—with its emphasis on Greek Revival and continental influences—surpassed all previous efforts in grandeur and size. Space was no longer a problem.

Neighborhoods grew in separate clumps on adjacent plantations. The layout of the individual plantations strongly affected the neighborhoods that sprang up on its grounds. Beautiful, high-ceilinged homes, with many windows looking out on gracious gardens, took over the open areas around each plantation's main house. Even the servants' quarters developed, but they became rather unimpressive "fringe" sections. New Orleans has kept this unique arrangement of grand homes bounded by lesser ones, and visitors can still see that almost every neighborhood reflects this same pattern. The present Garden District emerged as the principal and most impressive upriver residential area.

By the 1850s, the two strong cultures in New Orleans had finally begun to intermingle. Several lofty Garden District homes and a few in the Vieux Carré heralded this new unity. From this time on, marriages between Creoles and Americans were not uncommon, and, furthermore, most people were teaching their children to speak both French and English. The people of New Orleans were enjoying their happiest and most prosperous days just before the disaster of the Civil War.

BEAUREGARD HOUSE
1113 Chartres Street

THE BEAUREGARD HOUSE is one of the early Vieux Carré architectural contributions to the Golden Era in New Orleans (1830–60). Historically it is one of the city's most romantic houses, since the names of several famous persons have been linked—directly or indirectly—with its past. Confederate General Pierre Gustave Beauregard rented this house after the Civil War and his name has very obviously become permanently attached to the property.

Joseph Le Carpentier built the Beauregard House for his Creole wife, Modeste Blanche, and their four children. He had accumulated a great deal of money as a prominent auctioneer whose services were an integral part of Louisiana's plantation economy. Le Carpentier bought the grounds for his home from the Ursuline nuns when they decided to relocate in the suburbs and the old Ursuline convent can still be seen at 1114 Chartres Street—opposite the Beauregard House. After living there seven years, Le Carpentier sold his house to John Ami Merle, whose wife added lasting beauty to the grounds by planting a formal garden in an unused front corner of the lot.

Daily life of the early owners probably differed very little from other Creole families. Meals were prepared in a separate kitchen house behind the rear parterre and hot dishes were rushed by nimble servants through the parterre, up the stairs, and onto the table. Sunday breakfast was often an exceptional affair, for guests invited by after Mass frequently stayed past midnight. The meal was usually elaborate and would have included such dishes as: morning bitters; fresh fruit compote; breakfast salad; hot oyster cocktail; kidneys in wine or beef grillades; hominy or grits; beaten biscuits; café au lait (coffee with milk) or French chocolate; rosé wine; brandy.

The Beauregard House was erected in 1826 with James Lambert as builder and François Correjolles as architect. It is done on a grand scale in the

Figure 1 Beauregard House

Paladian style. A wide front gallery is reached from the street by gracefully curved double stairs. The stairs are not the original ones, but were probably added in the 1850s. Five principal rooms fitted with elegant moldings and marble mantles stand on either side of the central hallway on the main floor. Of these, three bedrooms and the *salle de compagnie* (reception parlor) are exceptionally large, and the banquet room is a magnificent twenty-five by fifty feet. The ground floor, or basement, was used for storage, a wine cellar, and servants' quarters.

The Beauregard House, now owned by the Keyes Foundation, owes its restoration to the efforts of a group of concerned citizens and particularly to the financial aid of Frances Parkinson Keyes who for many years lived and wrote in the seclusion of its rooms.

HERMANN-GRIMA HOUSE
820 St. Louis St.

SAMUEL HERMANN, a German immigrant, arrived in New Orleans with his Creole wife, Marie Emeronthe Becnel Brou, after the War of 1812. He quickly achieved success as a commission merchant of international importance and established himself in elite New Orleans social circles. At the height of his career, in 1831, his family and fortune having grown, Hermann

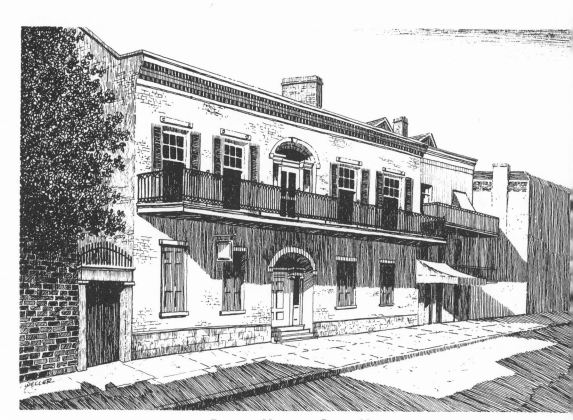

Figure 2 Hermann-Grima House

replaced his home on St. Louis Street in the Vieux Carré with one more opulent and in keeping with his grand way of life. The Hermann-Grima House is one of the finest examples of American influence on New Orleans architecture after the Louisiana Purchase.

William Brand, the best American builder of the times, drew up detailed specifications. The "marbelized" baseboards painted to match black marble mantels, doors finished in the faux-bois technique (painted woodgrain), and a hand-hewn drainage system for the flagstone courtyard reflected the owner's wealth, social position, and exacting taste.

Hermann took special pride in a separate three-story brick kitchen house with *garçonnière* (bachelor quarters). Kitchen equipment was the best available and included two fireplaces, the larger having an open hearth with every attachment, the other was built to accommodate a distinctive cast-iron baking oven with "stew holes"—a truly modern innovation for this early kitchen.

Foreign visitors and business associates were often entertained at elaborate soirées, and company dinners were lengthy, ceremonious affairs consisting of five to seven courses accompanied by different wines. No doubt on these occasions a liveried butler stood by the large sideboard and carved various dinner meats, while colorfully dressed servants passed the food and two Negro boys operated an overhead fan to keep away flies. The Hermanns had ice delivered to the house for these occasions—a real luxury, since at that time it had to be imported from far north.

After dinner, gentlemen would retire to the parlor, shut the door, and smoke. In Creole fashion, guests would perhaps be served *eau sucré*, sweetened water, to aid digestion, and all fine china, crystal, and silver used at the meal would be safely arranged to await a time when Madame Hermann herself could wash each piece. This was a necessary precaution in days when tableware patterns were not easily replaced.

This utopia did not last however, for Hermann suffered great financial losses and by 1844 his grand home was sold to Felix Grima, a wealthy notary. Today the Hermann-Grima House, now owned by the Christian Woman's Exchange, has been restored as authentically as possible to its original elegance.

GALLIER HOUSE
1132 Royal Street

JAMES GALLIER, Jr., following in his father's footsteps, became one of the foremost architects in New Orleans during the nineteenth century. His home at 1132 Royal Street, though comparatively small for a great house of the time, is a fine example of the Anglo-American style.

Gallier arrived in New Orleans early in the 1850s. His architectural background had been established in his native England, later in New York, and under the influence of his father. He was soon in partnership with Richard Esterbrook and John Turpin. These young men are credited with many architectural triumphs in New Orleans. Among these are the historical French Opera House (destroyed by fire in 1919); Forstall House, 920 St. Louis Street; the Luling Mansion on Leda and Esplanade Avenue; and the Episcopal House, 2265 St. Charles Avenue.

In 1857, Gallier designed and built his home practically behind the Beauregard House. He was then a young professional man supporting his wife and four daughters. Gallier had married Aglae Villavaso, a Creole girl who had been raised on a sugar plantation in St. Bernard Parish.

The Gallier House is important for many reasons—the foremost being that it was built by an architect for his own use. Its design and decorative detail are based on textbook motifs following classical European styles of that day. This approach was the basis of American and English architecture in the 1850s for the Greek Revival influence was, for the time, out of vogue.

Such a house stood in great contrast to its surroundings in the Vieux Carré—a section which continued essentially in early French traditions. No doubt the Gallier homesite was chosen in deference to the Creole Madame Gallier's wishes.

Guests must have been intrigued by the Gallier's home. It had ventilators upstairs disguised as ceiling medallions, closet space (a unique idea), a cast-iron stove in the kitchen, and an icebox in the back foyer. Water ran

Figure 3 Gallier House

from spiggots in a kitchen sink and the family enjoyed the novel luxury of a bathroom with tub, sink, and toilet! This in a day when, to most people, running water meant a hydrant in the yard, and the only sinks were the gutters of the streets and gardens.

New Orleans streets were still unsightly and made a poor playground for children. Gallier must have considered his family when he included a central grassy plot in their otherwise formal paved courtyard. While children played there, Aglae Gallier could sit chatting, sewing, and sipping lemonade with her Creole friends. Perhaps the little girls would be called on to perform for their mother's guests. It is possible that the crashing chords of *Battle of the Prague* resounded on occasion through the open windows of the house.

Members of the Gallier family sold the property in 1917. Today the house is owned by the Freeman Foundation. The structure and furnishings of the house have been accurately restored.

LA MOTHE HOUSE
621 Esplanade Avenue

IT IS BELIEVED that two brothers, Jean and Pierre La Mothe, arrived in Louisiana from Santo Domingo in the late eighteenth century and, quickly adjusting to the prevailing culture, established themselves as plantation owners in St. Charles Parish. Eventually, the La Mothes built a town house on Esplanade Avenue, near the Mississippi River, on the edge of old Faubourg Marigny. This house, designed to serve the needs of two families, is a "double" with two front entranceways. It is one step up from the banquette (sidewalk) and rises three stories high. Still known as La Mothe House despite the passage of time, the house remains a neighborhood landmark.

The floor plan throughout is simple, with double parlors on either side of a common central hall. Narrow two-story wings extend from the back, creating a central parterre (garden). These wings probably served as bachelor quarters above and service rooms below. The parlors downstairs were decorated with a restrained elegance which does not appear on the upper floors. Crystal chandeliers, double-leaded overdoors, and black marble mantels provided an elaborate background for the crowded soirées and dinner parties that were so much a part of the La Mothe's city life.

Planters and their families arrived annually in New Orleans aboard the river packets, always in time for the November opening of the opera. Once settled in their winter quarters, they remained until spring when the threat of oncoming summer epidemics and the needs of their plantations sent them home. The families no doubt considered New Orleans' winter season a gay relief from the routine of plantation life. Walking through muddy streets was no deterrent to Creole social activities, and many a belle arrived at a ball or the theater by foot—barefoot—with a little *cocodri* (Negro boy) in tow, carrying his mistress's shoes.

Figure 4 La Mothe House

The La Mothes lived close enough to the Vieux Carré to enjoy its conveniences and even the marchandes (street vendors) with large baskets balanced on their heads, were apt to appear on Esplanade selling their wares. A shout to a vendor, and for breakfast one might secure a delicious heart-shaped cream cheese with a dash of cream, a portion of *calas tout chauds*, or perhaps articles from the shop of the marchande's owner. It was not unusual for frugal Creole ladies to take advantage of street vending by sending their own servants out to sell violets, figs, candied orange slices, or other delicacies from home gardens and kitchens.

The history of La Mothe House is not clearly recorded but eventually it became rental property. It is operated today by Mrs. Edward P. Munson, a most gracious hostess, who runs it as a small hotel accommodating visitors to New Orleans.

PITOT HOUSE
1370 Moss Street

DESPITE the surrounding residential sprawl of New Orleans, the Pitot House stands facing quiet Bayou St. John, its architectural integrity uncompromised by the passage of years. At the time this simple plantation-style home was built, it stood on thirty acres stretching two hundred feet along the Bayou. Woodlands, meadows, and many fruit trees enhanced the grounds and gardens. The house was built in 1799 by Don Bartolome Bosque, and in 1810, James Pitot became its third owner. Other homes of this genre can be seen at 924 Moss Street and 1300 Moss Street.

The Pitot House is a two-story structure reflecting a West Indian influence. Wide galleries shade living quarters on both levels, and a back "cabinet" gallery (one with a small closet at each end) holds the only stairway. The graceful structure is crowned by the traditional French colonial hipped roof. Though not spacious, somehow the entire Pitot family managed to live and sleep in the upper three rooms. They probably dined downstairs in the coolness of the ground floor and, mosquitoes permitting, used the galleries as open air parlors. Outbuildings such as the kitchen, servants' and fowl houses, stable, carriage house and barn, provided working room for the servants.

James Pitot was an industrious French Creole who left his mark on the early development of New Orleans and his name forever on the Pitot House. He was appointed mayor of the city in 1804, and in 1813 was made a city and parish judge. During his judgeship, Pitot lived in the Moss Street house and regularly traveled Bayou Road, entering New Orleans through the Rampart Street gate.

Madame Pitot, following Creole custom, seldom would have left her home during the day and probably spent many leisure hours sitting on the front galleries, watching the busy bayou activities. Boats carrying goods of all kinds crowded the waters and Fanny, the Pitot's cook, had only to step out

Figure 5 Pitot House

of the door and march to the bayou's edge to secure ingredients for the family's meals.

Seafoods of salt- and fresh-water varieties, wild game, and Indian seasonings could all be bought from the bayou market boats, while barrels of wine, champagne, and other imported items were purchased on Pitot's frequent trips to New Orleans. Meals often included soups and stews composed of leftovers, for Madame Pitot, like other Creole housewives, threw nothing edible away. Gumbos of meats, poultry, or seafood were filling dishes and stretched a long way when unexpected guests were present.

Now owned by the Louisiana Landmarks Society, the Pitot House has been repositioned on the property and is being restored. It stands today strangely aloof from its surroundings. Gone are the fruit trees, gardens, and outbuildings, but the house itself appears much as it did in colonial days.

TOBY-WESTFELDT HOUSE
2340 Prytania Street

AS NEW ORLEANS expanded, and upriver plantation lands were developed into sprawling suburbs, the city's lovely Garden District was established on what was once the Livaudais sugar plantation. The Toby-Westfeldt House is one of the most charming homes in that area. It was built in 1838, by Thomas Toby on a lot at the corner of First and Prytania Streets. Shaded by huge live oak trees and surrounded by sugar-cane fields, this raised cottage with a white picket fence soon became a reference point to residents. Its location is still called Toby's Corner.

This house displays the most appealing aspects of Louisiana plantations and Creole traditions. However, the flat roof and floor plan suggest that no architect was contracted to draw formal plans.

A wide front stairway originally led to the open galleries of the main floor. Six bedrooms allowed the Toby family more privacy than that seen in most large homes of the day. The ground floor is of typical brick-piered construction and held a number of rooms including the dining room and summer parlors. During Toby's tenure, the grounds covered an entire city block, with outbuildings serving as kitchen, stable, and servants' quarters.

Thomas Toby was a man of great vitality and social standing. He established the largest wheelwright business in the South, became one of the city's most successful commission merchants, and over the years held important civic positions. In the 1830s, as official agent for Texas in the area, he was deeply involved in the Texas rebellion against Mexico, and he suffered severe financial losses when the Alamo fell.

Toby's family was greatly affected by his intense love for his country. This is seen in the names he chose for some of his eleven children. There was Louisiana Clara, Texas Henry, Indiana Delphine, Alabama Emily, Carolina Clemens, and Virginia Frances. It is a sad fact that only seven of the Toby children lived to maturity.

Madame Toby, Eliza Clemence Augustin, was a Creole and, no doubt, ran her household according to the dictates of that society. Her motherly duties would have included mixing lip salve, face powder, and hair pomade for herself and her daughters. Although she was probably less homebound than earlier Creole matrons, with her seamstress and daughters, Madame Toby would have been expected to sew clothes for the entire family and, in general, keep the furnishings of the house in good repair.

Renovations to the Toby house have resulted in changes to the entrance and stairs, and the addition of new galleries and a wing. In 1849, Toby's widow sold the house to the Westfeldt family, whose descendants live there today.

Figure 6 Toby-Westfeldt House

PAYNE-STRACHAN HOUSE
1134 First Street

THE MAJESTIC PAYNE-STRACHAN HOUSE is a classic example of Greek Revival architecture, and its charm is enhanced by its brief but romantic brush with history. It was built during the American architectural boom in the suburbs of New Orleans. Like that of Thomas Toby, it stands on property which was originally part of the Livaudais Plantation. In the 1840s and 1850s, land in this area sold for much less than sections nearer the Vieux Carré. Here impressive homes often appeared in country settings with spacious grounds and gardens.

Jacob U. Payne was born in Kentucky, came to Louisiana and eventually built a cotton plantation, Barbreck, in St. Landry Parish and a home on First and Camp Streets in New Orleans. He was married to Charlotte Downs from Vicksburg, Mississippi, had three children, and was generally assessed as a strong-minded individual and an astute businessman. Payne never gave up control of Barbreck, but the majority of his time was spent in New Orleans, where he worked long hours as a commission merchant dealing principally in cotton and sugar.

The house is dated in the early 1850s. Lack of records indicating an architect or builder makes it very probable that Payne himself chose ideas and plans from widely used illustrated builders' guidebooks. It is also probable that labor for the building and timber for the cypress beams and heart pine floors were brought to the city from Barbreck.

The Payne-Strachan House has double front balconies with handsome columns, Ionic below, Corinthian above, and cast iron capitals marked New York, 1848. Plaster work is done with effective simplicity and ceiling medallions are not limited to the parlors. The house has several "dep" windows which are unique and serve as doorways when a wood panel beneath them is opened.

The Paynes took great pride in this house, furnishing the parlors with

Figure 7 Payne-Strachan House

modish Victorian pieces complete with heavy velvet draperies. In New Orleans, however, all windows were thrown open so that sun and light could brighten the festive occasion of New Year's Day. Nineteenth-century New Orleanians considered New Year's a day set aside for visiting and receiving. Starting at 11:30 in the morning, all brothers, fathers, and grandfathers donned their finest clothes, adjusted their "stovepipes" (tall silk hats), and sallied forth to fulfill their yearly social obligation. The ladies in each house, primped for the occasion, arranged refreshments and awaited their callers. In the late evening, after leaving their cards at perhaps fifty homes where they had politely sampled fifty different cakes and eggnog mixtures, or sipped fifty less varied brandies or straight whiskies, overindulged gentlemen tottered gratefully home to their beds.

The Payne-Strachan House has outlasted this hospitable custom and its beauty has only been enhanced through the years by the careful efforts of its owners.

After the Civil War, the house passed to Payne's son-in-law, Charles E. Fenner, and it was during that time that Judge Fenner's friend Jefferson Davis, former President of the Confederacy, died in a downstairs bedroom. The house is now owned by Mr. and Mrs. Frank Strachan.

THE PLANTATION HOUSES
OF LOUISIANA

AN EERIE MARSH, a land of green flocking sprinkled over still, dark water—a dip of the wing and the jet-age traveler is introduced to Louisiana. It is a strange land, this lake-studded fringe of the state. It makes one think of the Greek Limbo, where lost souls wander mournfully through the gray mists. Yet there is something about the marshlands that is oddly thrilling; for this swamp, this land eaten away by the great river that drains the tremendous Mississippi Valley from the far north to the sea, this is what heroic explorers saw over four hundred years ago, when they forced their way up the Mississippi to open the rich valley lands for colonization. DeSoto, LaSalle, Iberville, Bienville—the names of these men are familiar to school-children everywhere, and rightly so, for their efforts resulted in the development of a region that today offers a unique contribution to America. Louisiana, with its wealth of birds and fur-bearing animals, oil and gas, swampland and pine woods, is today a mélange of two cultures, the European and the American, and all through the state the old ways and customs are cherished and revered.

Louisiana is not only a mixture of two cultures; it is two different regions, as well. Looking at a map of the state, you see a shape like a ragged boot, the sole and toe worn away by the Gulf and its powerful agent, the Mississippi. At the top of the boot, the northwest corner of the state was covered by a vast stand of virgin oak trees when the first settlers arrived in Louisiana. The virgin forests fell before the timberman's ax long ago, but the rich soil that oak trees betoken is still there, and its fertility played a part in the settling of the state. In the center of the state, in Vernon, Rapides, and half of Calcasieu Parish stood piney woods, as in the parishes across Lake Pontchartrain from New Orleans. In these areas, where the soil is not so rich, the air is clear and fresh, and flowering plants that love light, acid soil—the camellias, azaleas, and the cape jasmine that Louisianians call gardenias—

grow in abundance everywhere. In the center of the foot part of the boot the explorers found a prairie area, where the Attakapas Indians dwelt, a brave and handsome race. But the greatest wealth in the soil lies in the alluvial lands on either side of the Mississippi River, the true delta of this brown river, for the alluvial lands stretch from Carroll Parish in the northeast of the state, and run down on either side as the river flows to the Gulf. The soil is incredibly fertile, and the names of the sugar parishes (parish is the old ecclesiastical term Louisiana uses instead of county) trip off the tongue like a magic formula: Ascension, Assumption, St. James, St. Mary, Terrebonne; to cite a few. These are the lands where sugar cane sways, growing tall and sweet in the Louisiana sun, producing half of the sugar raised in the state. The northern alluvial parishes and the central parishes grow cotton, soybeans, and tobacco.

Water is the key to the richness of these lands, water and people are the key, in fact, to much of Louisiana's special place in history and unusual characteristics today. Water: rainfall, floods, rivers, streams, and slow-moving bayous; the yawning Gulf of Mexico, the water-worn tip of the state, the lakes—water in its many shapes is responsible for much of the state's glamorous past and especially for the development of the plantations.

In the spring, before the Americans came to harness the mighty Mississippi, floodwaters spilled over the banks of the river and submerged the surrounding lands. When the waters receded, a valuable deposit remained. In some spots in Louisiana, the rivers and bayous are actually higher than the surrounding land and flow between ridges they themselves have built up over the centuries. Even the earliest French and Spanish colonials recognized the need for control of the waterways. Mounds of earth called levees were thrown up to guard the towns, the farms, and the plantations. In the early days, at the end of the eighteenth and the first part of the nineteenth centuries, the levees were makeshift affairs, ranging in height from five to fifty feet. It took a long time for a levee to take hold, nearly five years, and the levees were always threatened—the plantation folk especially lived in fear of a crevasse—a break in the levee.

Many are the great houses that have fallen to the flood, in one way or another. Uncle Sam Plantation, for instance, lay on the east bank of the Mississippi River, between New Orleans and Baton Rouge. In 1844, Pierre Auguste Samuel Fagot began the erection of a collection of buildings in the Greek Revival style. When the buildings were completed, in 1850, the *tout ensemble*, as Louisianians say, was the most imposing on the river. Two garçonnières, kitchen buildings, plantation office, and classic peaked-roof pigeonnières reflected the Doric-columned style of the manor. Stables, hospital, and a long line of slave quarters, the traditional two-room, single-chimneyed structures, marched from the main area to the imposing sugar-house, the heart of the plantation. These buildings, each a jewel of its type, remained intact until 1947. They had escaped the ravages of war and survived the scourge of the elements. But the Mississippi River had been slowly moving toward the heart of Uncle Sam. The levee was moved, strengthened, moved again, to no avail. Finally, the only possible course of containment was a new and mightier levee, right where the big house had stood for nearly one hundred years. And so the plantation was destroyed, torn down, the end of the dream of Samuel Fagot, whose brooding ambition had given rise to the finest collection of buildings on the river.

Today, the great river is harnessed, but the bindings that restrain it must constantly be renewed. People who live in the lower Mississippi Valley live in vigilance; there are drainage ditches to be kept clear, streams to be dredged, levees to be maintained. The beautiful water hyacinth, a Japanese import that escaped from the Cotton Centennial Exposition in 1885, must be battled to prevent its taking over the navigable streams. Twice each year, at high water in the spring and low water in the fall, the Mississippi River Commission sends a boat down the river. It stops at the little towns, and the planters of today come to work out the problems that have beset men on the river since the first Indian put foot in the valley thousands of years ago.

The Mississippi and its many little sister rivers made possible the development of Louisiana by acting as a great net of roadways throughout the state. Men sailed and paddled up the river and floated down with the swift current until, in January of 1812, the *New Orleans* became the first steamboat to navigate the Mississippi. For almost sixty years, the steamboats plied the rivers; the great boats carrying people and goods, the small packet boats carrying mail and packages, visitors and slaves from city to country, from plantation to plantation. Until the 1870s, when the Iron Horse of the railroad ended its reign, the steamboat was an important part of the glorious days of the old plantation life.

Traveling up the Mississippi on a steamboat in the 1840s and '50s was an experience unequaled in the rest of America, for the plantations, resembling miniature medieval fiefdoms, slipped past the wide-eyed visitors one after another, each seemingly more splendid than the last. From Point Coupée above Baton Rouge to New Orleans, the grand mansions passed in review, majestic, compelling, the expression of a life style that seemed to be so solid as to last forever, and yet, one that existed only for a short half-century before it vanished into oblivion.

The plantation houses themselves represent an architectural development that is very different from most of the architecture in the rest of America. The first settlers, the French and Spanish, whose children called themselves Creoles, built their simple homes out of a plaster made of mud mixed with Spanish moss, the exquisite air plant that to this day adorns the oaks of the state. The plaster was spread between vertical posts of cypress, a wood that resists the ever-present dampness as well as the ubiquitous termite. This mixture of mud and wood is called *bousillage entre poteaux*. As the years have rolled on, it has become extremely hard, and in its hardened condition, it represents an obstacle to modern restoration, for the plumbers and electricians find it difficult to penetrate. The early Creole cottages were covered with hipped roofs that swept from their high peaks to overhang wide verandas, called galleries, and to provide protection from the heavy rain and sun. The water table was very close to the surface of the ground, and so the Creoles raised their houses off of the ground a half story. The water table had another interesting side effect: to the horror of the early settlers, coffins holding the bodies of the dead burst out of the ground as a result of the drenching tropical rains, and so the graveyards were built with raised tombs, sometimes called ovens. These vaults often contain many generations of a family, and many of them remain, especially in New Orleans, where Roman Catholic families make a practice of white-washing their family tombs and decorating them with flowers on All Saints' Day.

The settlers' increasing affluence enabled them to construct larger and finer homes. The floor plan was changed; a central hall ran between high-ceilinged rooms, allowing for better circulation of summer breezes. A second floor was added, reached by staircases fit for the mistress of the place to sweep down in splendor to greet her many guests, for the plantation people were famed for their hospitality. They entertained a steady stream of relatives, friends, and travelers, who, passing by boat or barge, often stopped at a convenient plantation, there being no inns along the way.

Between 1820 and 1830, Louisiana planters began to establish great fortunes in sugar and cotton. Many of them were now of Anglo-Saxon stock, for the Americans had emigrated into the state with the Louisiana Purchase in 1803. The Americans were dominant in the "upper toe" of the Louisiana boot, the so-called Florida parishes, which joined the Union in 1810. The Creoles were Roman Catholics, and their influence prevailed in the rest of the foot. With their sometimes bumptious vitality, the Americans, like their Creole rivals, accumulated great fortunes, and they began to spend it on their houses, with often pretentious results! Greek Revival, the influence of which was felt throughout the South, had great impact in Louisiana. The massive pillars, the great entabulatures, the wide, cool galleries, the tremendous rooms—bedrooms so large, says one early correspondent, that it was a journey to travel across to the armoire—all of these things were a part of the palaces that sprang up along the rivers.

John Randolph, a son of one of the Virginia Randolphs, hired the famous architect Henry Howard to build himself a great white castle he called Nottaway, fifty rooms, one of which was a tremendous round ballroom— since John Randolph had been blessed with eight daughters for whom he had to find husbands. His next-door neighbor, another American named Andrews, responded by building his own castle, a fifty-eight-room, pink *palazzo* dubbed Belle Grove, to draw the dazzled eyes away from Nottaway. Nottaway still stands outside of Plaquemine in Iberville Parish. A mammoth brick house covered with cement, its square wooden pillars rise two stories tall above a raised ground floor.

Enormous fortunes were made in sugar, though it was not the first staple crop in Louisiana; the early settlers had cultivated indigo. Indigo required a care in growing that the slaves were not readily able to develop, and in 1793, a plague of caterpillars wreaked havoc on the plantations for three years, causing most of the Creole planters to abandon indigo. Then in 1795, one of the most exciting events in the history of agriculture in America took place on the well-ordered and beautiful plantation of Etienne de Boré, the site of which is now New Orleans' Audubon Park. De Boré had decided that the commercial cultivation of sugar cane would solve Louisiana's agricultural problems, and that he would make a major investment in sugar. His land was broken early in the year, and the roots, or ratoons, from which the cane grows, were laid end to end. All through the spring and the long, hot, wet summer, the slaves hoed the weeds away from the growing cane, while the stalks grew tall and thickened with the sweet juice. The frost, devastating to cane, held off; the cane was harvested in the fall and carried to De Boré's sugarhouse, where it was ground and the extracted juice ladled into a battery of huge black iron sugar kettles. As the boiling process proceeded, the slaves and their owners crowded around, until at last the moment they had been praying for arrived: a cry went up, it granulated! and Louisiana's future was set. De Boré was the first man in what is now the United States to succeed in granulating sugar on a commercial scale; he made $12,000 from that first crop, and the Louisiana planters rushed to emulate him. They affectionately tagged him "The Savior of Louisiana."

By the 1840s and '50s, life on the sugar plantations had fallen into a distinctive pattern. Slaves were essential to the sugar crop; they represented a large investment on the part of the owners, and they were so expensive that only half of the whites in Louisiana were slave owners. The prices of slaves rose sharply after 1808, for the United States banned further importation. The slaves worked in "gangs" in the fields; rising with the sun to eat a simple breakfast, they went immediately to the fields where they worked until midday. In the heat of the summer, they were often given two hours off at midday to eat and rest, and they returned to the fields to work until evening. The harvest began with the cane cutting; the slaves toiled down the long rows of tall cane until they had harvested all but the final row. When the final row was reached, the foreman, *le commandeur*, chose the best laborer from among the gangs to be proclaimed *le meilleur couteau*. The *commandeur* selected the tallest cane from the last row, and tied a shining blue ribbon around it. The knife was handed to le meilleur couteau, who brandished the knife and danced about the cane stalk, singing to it as if it were a person. Finally, with much ceremony, the last stalk was cut, and borne in triumph by le meilleur couteau to the big house, where the planter, the mistress, and the children of the house crowded about to see. A great cheer rang up as the slaves presented the beribboned stalk; the master of the plantation toasted his slaves; and all hands were given a drink. At harvest time, the hours for the slaves were longer, and when the grinding began in the sugar house, gangs worked around the clock, while the towering chimney of the sugarhouse sent out a steady stream of bluish smoke, letting the travelers on the river know that the sugar making was proceeding apace. During grinding, life was exciting for the whole plantation, however, regardless of the hard work—there was a sense of festivity in the air, and the slaves were frequently supplied with drinks.

Holidays for the slaves were Sundays; the Black Code, promulgated by Bienville in 1724, required that they be given instruction in the Catholic faith, and the Sabbath was strictly observed. Many plantation owners gave the slaves a half a day off on Saturday, too, to wash their clothes and make themselves presentable for Mass or for church services. The slaves were usually encouraged by their owners to raise fruits, vegetables, and poultry, and the owners bought their produce. On some of the plantations, a festival was held in the fall around hog-killing time, but for all of the plantations, New Year's Day was the high point of the year. On New Year's Day, the slaves were given their presents; a suit, or two, if the owner was generous; a hat; a new dress or two for the women, with an extra dress for each woman who had borne a child during the preceding year. Sometimes the gifts included a tin plate and a spoon, and a small sum of money.

The life of a slave was one of toil and drudgery, and the facts of bondage are not pleasant. Yet the slaves in Louisiana in the 1840s and '50s, during the peak of the plantation days, were healthier and their lives more pleasant than that of the poor white farmers who made up more than half the white population. A slave was valuable to his owner, and so the owner cared for him. Most of the plantations paid a doctor a small annual fee to visit and pass out advice concerning health care several times a year, and the mistress of the plantation frequently supervised the care of the sick herself, with the aid of a medical book of the times. The plantation owners were careful about the purity of the water they drank, too; they collected the abundant rainfall in great cisterns and checked its cleanliness. The farmers on their small plots took their water from wells sunk in the ground, and so they were sometimes the victims of typhoid as well as a host of other ailments.

The plantation owner who ran his own plantation was a hard-working man; his wife, mistress of the nearly self-sufficient community the plantation represented, worked almost as hard as he. One of the hardest-working, most successful, and innovative of the plantation owners was a proud Creole named Valcour Aimé, whose fabulous plantation in St. James Parish was often compared to Versailles. His experiments with sugar cane, with methods of sugar making, with the new power offered the sugar planters by the use of steam—all these led to the great success of his business enterprise, and gave him the money with which to support his more expensive and exotic interests, for Valcour Aimé was actually an ardent amateur botanist. He sent all over the world for rare plants with marvelous flowers, and soon the gardens about his house were the talk of the South. The landscaping, done after the fashion of Europe in his day, centered around several small parks, a little wood with a mixture of animals; rabbits, a deer, a number of kangaroos; a fort for the children's games; and a small hill ten feet high, upon which stood a Chinese pagoda, the top festooned with little bells that rang in the slightest wind. But in 1853, with the death from yellow fever of his one, too beloved son, the life of Valcour Aimé came to its official close. He ended the diary of thirty years of productive life that is still a record of fascination to those who are interested in the plantations, and the plantation itself slipped rapidly into decay.

The plantation owners and the houses that they built represent a brief epic that in its sophistication and its opulence is unmatched in the annals of American history. The Creole inheritance of French culture and tradition gave to the planters, American as well as Creole, an appreciation of the beautiful and a solid foundation in taste. Their taste, their instinctively correct response to beauty as opposed to the gaucherie that often typifies the reaction of a newly rich class, is a distinguishing quality of the plantation houses, the lives of the people, and their management of their world.

Only the rich could afford alluvial lands and slaves, the rest of the rural population lived on farms. In 1850, although the plantations took up seven times the land area of the farms, only two out of five agricultural holdings were plantations. The farms had some common characteristics: they were small, their owners usually possessed no slaves; and they were generally single-crop operations. In the latter, they differed greatly from the plantations, which prided themselves on being self-sufficient. Living in a climate and on land that should have made them veritable cornucopias of plenty, the small farmers were sometimes without milk and hogs, so single-minded was their devotion to the corn, sugar, cotton, or tobacco that supported their meager existence.

The farmers themselves came of two different stocks. In the uplands, in the north of the state, dwelt the Americans who had pushed in after the Louisiana Purchase. Anglo-Saxon, Protestant, often poor, their lives were not markedly different from those of their kindred all over the antebellum South. But in the south of the state, on the second river-bottom lands, tucked away along the bayous, there lived another group of farmers, people whose descendants today live in a distinctly French ambiance. These people are the "Cajuns," and their history is long and colorful. Their ancestors, loyal Frenchmen, were driven from Acadia, or Nova Scotia, by the English and the Americans, who saw in their presence in the North a French threat to the expanding Anglo-American colonies. Large numbers of Acadians were deported in 1755, and after a series of tragic misadventures, the survivors arrived in Louisiana as settlers, to be followed by their confreres for the next thirty years. They were heartily welcomed by the French, Catholic Louisianians, and they soon made a place for themselves in the state. They lived in Louisiana as they had lived in Acadia; for they were simple folk whose needs were few, and who were always ready to dance and sing. They fell in love with the ample Louisiana waterways and developed their own version of the canoe, the pirogue, a small, knife-shaped boat that they manage with great skill and deftness even today: pirogue races are held every spring and fall. They became shrimp and oyster fishermen, and to this day, the archbishop comes out from New Orleans in his miter and flowing robes to bless the shrimp fleet, to wish the fishermen Godspeed. Their simple houses are like the wooden houses their ancestors built two centuries ago. An outside staircase to reach the sleeping quarters is testimony to Cajun thrift, for a two-story house with only an outside staircase was considered for tax purposes only a one-story structure! Cajun girls have smooth olive skins and dark hair; their accent is a rich, strange blend of French and English. To this day, one may turn on the radio near Breaux Bridge, on Bayou Teche, famed for its crawfish dishes, and hear French-speaking announcers and pitchmen. Cajuns have a great sense of the comic; late in the evening, many a smooth-spoken, highly educated raconteur will reveal by a sudden lapse into dialect and a wild gust of humor the Cajun blood that burns in his veins. The Cajuns are folk who have lived in poverty since the early days; they arrived with nothing, they have few of the materialistic cravings that burden many Americans, and they inherited a French custom of parceling out ancestral land among all of the male children. Since the Cajuns are remarkably prolific, their land holdings have a tendency to get smaller with succeeding generations rather than larger. But they are a gay, happy people, at home in their world, enjoying *la vie* to the hilt in their native parishes.

Up the Cane River, near Natchitoches (pronounced Nak-a-tosh), lives another group of people whose history is the stuff of romance. This settlement, one of the oldest in the Mississippi River Valley, was developed in part by free people of color; they were slaves who had been set free or who had bought their own freedom, or the free children of the liaisons between the French colonials and the beautiful black women who were their mistresses. Many of these children were quite fair, and were well educated; often given sums of money by their fathers, they settled around the Cane River, where their descendants still live today. One of the most glamorous of these people was a woman, Marie Therese Coin Coin. Born in the Congo, brought to America as a small child, she was set free after the death of her master, and given a grant of land by the French Crown. She prospered greatly, first selling the virgin timber from her land, then cultivating indigo, and she made enough money to buy her daughter and grandchild out of slavery, and to build her own, very different plantation. Her home, Yucca, used the Creole *bousillage entre poteaux,* and other buildings on the place are said to be the only American examples of African architecture that date from colonial times. Eventually, the plantation fell into the hands of the whites who moved into the Cane River area; the name was changed from Yucca to Melrose, and until 1970, the plantation remained occupied and working. Now, the house stands empty, its fabulous collection of antiques auctioned off. The ghosts of its black and white masters seem to drift mournfully through the enormous pecan grove on the place, grieving that the house they built may join the other bony skeletons and piles of vine-crowned ashes that alone remain of other men's dreams of magnificence.

There were, of course, other people whose ways and language and customs have given a special touch to Louisiana. There are the Germans, who crowded in during the 1850s. Many of them died of yellow fever, but others came. Their names were changed, so that Creole tongues might twist about them better; Wagonsbeck, for example, became Waguespack; and a local chronicler, Charles Dufour, tells the hilarious story of one Johann Zweig. His desperate efforts to give his name to the immigration official who spoke no German resulted in his being given the name Jean LaBranche! The Germans settled with the Irish in the slums of New Orleans, or pushed on into the countryside where they founded the town known today as Des Allemands—Germantown. There were the Irish, whose exploitation during the 1840s and '50s is a source of shame. Living in squalor, they worked under conditions so dreadful that Negro slaves were not permitted to work alongside them—the risk of death for the valuable slave was too great for slaveowners to chance it. And there were the Indians, those first Americans who are so often last, even today. The Natchez, the brave and handsome Attakapas who were rumored to feast upon their enemies, the Choctaws, quarrelsome, not famous for cleanliness, but whose highest virtue was truth; the Tensas, overrun by their fellows, the Houmas—these all were decimated by the usual means. Disease, trickery, warfare; most of them finally joined the great exodus to Oklahoma, which the Choctaw language named Okla (red), Homma (people). Their shades remain in Louisiana, in the name of a great highway, Chef Menteur, chief liar—so-called because the truth-telling Choctaws drove away from their campfires that repugnant sport among them, a man who twists the truth. Indian mounds dot the landscape; one is at Melrose in the Cane River area. Archaeologists' digs turn up curious pottery, and other shards from the long-ago and peaceful days before Iberville and Bienville sailed up the muddy Mississippi.

Water—water, and people. These make Louisiana what it is. Although much has slipped away from us that men thought would last for centuries, much remains. And in the drowsing plantation houses, hugging the banks of the streams that made them possible, you can see the visible reminder of a time and a people in which an epic splendor, a great elegance, paused for a fleeting moment, almost like a beautiful dream caught in the mind before morning.

SAN FRANCISCO

On River Road (East Bank) Louisiana Highway 942,
About 2½ miles above Reserve
Open daily—Fee

ABHORRING the Greek Revival plantations that lined the Mississippi like stark white tombs, Valsin Marmillion built San Francisco Plantation, one of the most unusual homes in South Louisiana. He was a lover of steamboats, and was guided by the feeling that a man's home should embody life's gay and happy memories. The extension of his fantasies was a plantation built to resemble the floating palaces that traveled the river. Intricately carved wood and ironwork, typical of the stately New Orleans homes, accentuated the horizontal lines and created the effect of a ship's deck. Twin stairways, reminiscent of the grand salons, rose to the main entrance located on the second floor. Nestled atop the third-floor ballroom with its tinted-glass windows was a belvedere resembling the crow's nest of a ship. When completed in 1850, San Francisco was a tribute to Marmillion's individualism.

To decorate the interior ceilings and walls he hired Dominique Canova, a cousin of Napoleon's favorite sculptor. The artist's labors are still visible today as soft scenes of cherubs and birds surrounded by delicate trelises and flowering bowers. The real tribute to Marmillion's imagination, the ballroom, which was to be lined with multicolored glass to reflect a kaleidoscope of color as the dancers passed, was never completed. The failure of his cane crop, poor health, and the financial worries of his 100,000-dollar mansion probably were all contributing factors to his death. As his troubles mounted, legend recalls his use of the expression *mon saint-frusquin,* a country French venacular expression meaning "my last red cent" to describe his home. This expression was "anglicized" and the plantation became known as San Francisco. His wife and two young daughters remained in the home until it was sold. Mourning customs and financial pressures probably prevented them from entertaining on the scale that Marmillion envisioned when the house was built.

Figure 8 San Francisco

As was the story of many of the sugar-cane kings, Marmillion had grown wealthy with the success of his sugar crops during the two decades before the Civil War. His father had built one of the first sugar mills in St. John the Baptist Parish and maintained a very influential position in New Orleans social circles. His plantation, the Columbia, was located just across the river from San Francisco. On a visit to New Orleans, Louis Philippe of France, as the Duc d' Orléans, was entertained at Columbia Plantation in a typically lavish southern style. When the meal was complete, as the story goes, the gold and silver used by the duke was dumped in the river, so that no one of lesser status could eat from the elegant tableware.

San Francisco is presently occupied by Mr. and Mrs. Clark Thompson. The home was restored in 1954 and filled to capacity with eighteenth- and nineteenth-century French and English furniture, china, and silver. The plantation functions once again as the elegant family home conceived by the imaginative M. Marmillion in 1850.

HOUMAS HOUSE

On River Road (East Bank) Louisiana Highway 942
Just above Burnside
Open daily—Fee

LANDSCAPED GARDENS, blooming magnolias, and age-old Louisiana oaks surround the small, elegantly simple plantation, Houmas House. Its name was derived from the Houmas Indians, who occupied the land prior to French colonization. The original two-story, four-room dwelling was built by Alexandre Latil, toward the end of the eighteenth century. Forty years later, the gracious Greek Revival manor house was built by John Smith Preston and his wife, who was the daughter of Revolutionary War hero, General Wade Hampton. They chose to preserve the original four-room dwelling by joining it to the plantation with an arched carriageway, which served as the main entrance during inclement weather. The plantation home of the Prestons, with its Doric columns, plastered brick walls, dormer windows, and graceful, open-air galleries, was a typical example of the large mansions that line the Mississippi. The one unusual feature of the home was the glass windowed belvedere atop the second story, reflecting the style of Preston's former Carolina home. The Prestons lived at Houmas House for over a decade, but talk of secession and Civil War prompted Preston to return to South Carolina and to public life as a state senator. He sold Houmas House to John Burnside for two million dollars, thereby making a very handsome profit on the 10,000 acres he had developed.

John Burnside was a very astute businessman, successful with every venture he attempted. As a young Irish immigrant, he so enchanted the wealthy Virginian Andrew Bierne that Bierne adopted him and sent him to New Orleans with his own son, Oliver, to set up a commercial dry-goods business. Oliver soon gave up, but John remained to establish a store on Canal Street. He conceived the idea of placing two conversation chairs at the entrance to his store, thereby encouraging customers to linger and chat. His interest and dedication to his customers and community affairs won him many friends, and a sizable bank account.

Figure 9 Houmas House

Though Burnside remained a bachelor, he had a large circle of friends whom he entertained frequently at Houmas House. One of his visitors was W. H. Russell, who described Burnside's early-morning ritual of the mint julep. As the guest arose, he was greeted with a glass of brandy, sugar, peppermint, and ice, the planters' potion guaranteed to ward off any climatic condition. Once the glass was empty, the servant arrived with a second. Assuming that one was able to finish two juleps before dining, the servant again appeared with a third and final julep and strict instructions from the master as to its pre-breakfast consumption. Surely, the infrequent guest must have marveled at this unusual custom.

As Burnside's fortune grew, he purchased additional acres of land. At one point, Houmas House Plantation had four sugarhouses, each with a separate planting unit and its own set of slaves. The slave quarters were attached to each sugarhouse in double rows of cottages. Behind the cottages there were coops for poultry, geese, turkey, and pigs. Beyond the immediate confines of the slave quarters were small fields to be used by the slaves for their own planting. Possum hunts, fish fries, and church gatherings were their common forms of entertainment.

After Burnside's death, the plantation passed through several owners until Dr. George B. Crozat purchased the home. He directed the restoration to accentuate the home's original grace and simplicity. Many of its furnishings, such as his collection of Louisiana armoires, predate the Civil War. Also of interest is a map on the second floor which shows that Louis XIV, King of France, granted trading rights for all the land drained by the Mississippi to Antoine Crozat. What a coincidence that this land and lovely home should rest in the hands of a descendant of Monsieur Crozat.

ASPHODEL

On Louisiana Highway 68, off U. S. Highway 61
South of Jackson
Open weekdays; weekends by appointment—Fee

SEARCHING for virgin land, Benjamin Kendrick, a successful cotton planter, emigrated from Georgia to Louisiana. He selected a knoll in East Feliciana as the site of the modest manor house on his new cotton plantation, Asphodel. Begun in 1820, the house exemplifies the modified Greek Revival tradition adapted in Louisiana.

Sturdily constructed of brick, and plastered both inside and out, Asphodel is pleasing both in proportion and design. Two front rooms believed to have been used as double parlors open onto the front gallery and overlook the formal garden. No explanation can be found for the two front doors or the absence of a hall. The dining room and butlery open onto the back gallery, where servants hurried to and from the outside kitchen to serve the Kendricks and their guests. Wings to the left and right were probably added in 1833, and harmonize nicely with the original structure.

Upstairs the children lived more or less dormitory style with Clothilde, the nurse, sleeping outside their door. Privacy was not as important a consideration as it is today.

Plantation life was busy and idle hours were few. While Mr. Kendrick supervised his plantation, Mrs. Kendrick managed the household. Most often she could be found in her morning room adjoining the master bedroom. Here Mrs. Kendrick planned her menus and distributed the daily allotment of spices, coffee, and tea. The expensive spices, medicines, wines, and preserved foods were kept locked in the cellar, only a few steps from her bedroom door.

Recipes, though sparse in detail, were kept in a handwritten notebook. Imagination and memory were always a necessary ingredient as illustrated by the following recipe. Directions for Ginger Cake read: 1 cup butter, 2 cups molasses, 3 cups flour, 4 eggs, 1 teaspoon soda in ½ cup buttermilk, and add ginger if you like. Puddings of every kind were popular, whereas

Figure 10 Asphodel

tomatoes were considered unfit to eat and salad and raw greens were rarely used.

A major concern of the mistress was the health of her family and the 400–500 slaves living on the plantation, doctors being not only an additional expense but often living ten miles away. A popular cure for a sore throat Mrs. Kendrick no doubt used, was a gargle of salt and vinegar with a little cayenne pepper. It claimed to stimulate the glands, promote free secretion and further boasted to cure the throat in a few hours. It would be understandable, after undergoing this treatment, if the original complaint was entirely forgotten in a matter of minutes.

Today Asphodel is owned by Mr. and Mrs. Robert Couhig. An easy drive from New Orleans, food and lodging accommodations on the premises, plus close proximity to other interesting plantations, make a trip to Asphodel an enjoyable experience.

OAKLEY

On Louisiana Highway 965, off U. S. Highway 61,
About 4½ miles Southeast of St. Francisville
Open daily—Fee

OAKLEY was built on land obtained from a Spanish land grant by Ruffin Gray of Natchez. Uncertainty exists regarding the actual date of construction but the house is believed to have been completed in 1810; a year when West Feliciana was at successive intervals a Spanish possession, the West Florida Republic, and a United States territory. Oakley, today, is important both architecturally and historically.

Architecturally, it is simple in design, representing more the colonial style. It predates the Classic Revival period found in parts of nearby Rosedown. A decided West Indies influence is seen in the jalousied galleries which extend across the front and back, giving the house, in spite of its three stories, a light and airy feeling. Moldings of the simplest variety are to be found only in the parlor and library on the second floor, where guests were received. Medallions or other such embellishments are absent, although graceful, hand-carved Adams mantelpieces are present in all the major rooms. Visitors dined on the ground floor and food was kept hot in a warming oven in the adjoining room—a unique feature at the time.

Historically, it is renowned as having been the home for a brief period of John James Audubon. Mr. Gray died before Oakley's completion. His widow, the strong-willed Lucy Alston, married wealthy James Pirrie, a native of Scotland. On one of her frequent trips to New Orleans, Mrs. Pirrie hired Mr. Audubon and his young assistant, John Mason, as a tutor for her daughter, Eliza. During Audubon's short residence at Oakley Plantation, he completed thirty-two bird paintings by the time of his departure in 1821. More important, his love affair with his "Happyland" was well established. Audubon and his wife, would return at a later date, she to give lessons at neighboring Beech Woods, and he to paint and help the young ladies of the parish with their dancing. The courtesy and hospitality Audubon

Figure 11 Oakley

received from the local planters reflected the affluent and cultured society of the Feliciana parishes.

Eliza Pirrie is notable, too, in her own right. Gay and high-spirited, she must have made for some trying moments for the eccentric Mr. Audubon. Against her parents' wishes, Eliza became a June bride. In 1823, she eloped with her cousin, Robert Hilliard Barrow, of Highland Plantation. Unfortunately, while en route to Natchez, their carriage had to cross the Homochitto stream where the water was unusually high. Ever a gentleman, Robert carried Eliza across and returned to lead his team of horses through the waters. Six weeks later, the groom was dead from pneumonia, and his widow was left to raise their posthumously born son, Robert, Jr., alone. Five years passed and Eliza remarried, this time to the Reverend William Robert Bowman, the first rector of Grace Episcopal Church in St. Francisville. Their son, James Pirrie Bowman, would carry on family tradition by marrying another Feliciana belle, the beautiful Sarah Turnbull of Rosedown. Widowed again, the lovely Eliza remarried for the last time. She died at only forty-five and is buried next to the Reverend Bowman in Grace Church cemetery.

Oakley is owned by the State of Louisiana and to some is better known as Audubon Memorial State Park. It now comprises one hundred acres of land, and contains a wildlife sanctuary. Visitors may enjoy nature trails or picnicking under magnificent oak and magnolia trees. Perhaps, here, more than any other place, one gains a feeling for the unique quality of life enjoyed by pioneer cotton planters in this tiny outpost established by the Spanish crown.

ROSEDOWN

On Louisiana Highway 10, just off U. S. Highway 61,
North of St. Francisville
Open daily—Fee
Children under 12 years not permitted

ROSEDOWN, a plantation home set behind an avenue of live oak trees draped with Spanish moss, was built in 1834 by Daniel Turnbull. Mr. Turnbull was from nearby Catalpa Grove Plantation. He was well educated, financially astute, and one of the most successful Louisiana planters of his time. His brother-in-law, Bennett Barrow, probably described him best when he wrote: "saw Mr. Turnbull yesterday; the only independent man to be met—Fat and pockets full of money." In 1828, Daniel married Martha Barrow, daughter of one of the earliest Feliciana settlers, from North Carolina. Of their three children, only beautiful "Miss Sarah" survived her parents.

Rosedown is said to have been fashioned after Martha Turnbull's girlhood home, Highland Plantation. It is a well-balanced, two-storied house, constructed mainly of cypress with some cedar embellishments. Classic and stately in feeling, Rosedown has wide porches both up and down, supported by Doric columns extending across its front.

Two extensions with elaborate fluted columns were added ten years later to the right and left of the original building, and reflect the popularity in the Felicianas of the Greek Revival style. Added too, at a cost of $225.00, was a handsome Greek Revival gateway—an impressive entrance to greet the Turnbull's distinguished guests, among them, President Zachary Taylor.

To the front of the house and extending five acres on either side were Mrs. Turnbull's gardens. Obviously influenced by her trips abroad, Martha Turnbull, a remarkable amateur horticulturist, created her gardens patterned after the French style of the seventeenth century. To add importance, marble statues were imported from Italy. In these luxurious surroundings, rare plants and shrubs flourished along winding pathways and ornate little summer-houses. Today, these plants have grown to enormous size with camellias, azaleas, and other such shrubs now well over ten feet tall.

Figure 12 Rosedown

Surrounding the main house on some 3,455 acres, were the smaller buildings including Dr. King's office, quarters for Mr. Turnbull's 450 slaves with
a church and hospital for their personal use, barns, and outside kitchen,
and Mrs. Turnbull's conservatory.

The Turnbulls procured only the finest materials and furnishings for
Rosedown. Bookcases, handmade in France, and a mahogany bedroom suite

ordered from Prudent Mallard of New Orleans, one of America's leading cabinetmakers, were but a few of the treasures to travel the 150 miles up the Mississippi River to Bayou Sara and on by wagon to Rosedown. Scenic wallpaper, Carrara mantelpieces, brocaded draperies covering rose-point lace curtains and handpainted linen shades were still further evidence of Daniel Turnbull's affluence.

Life for the Turnbulls was not without *joie de vivre.* Trips to Europe, Saratoga, or White Sulphur Springs, were annual events and furnished a welcome respite from the hot summer months. En route to Saratoga, a visit to Philadelphia for portraits by Thomas Sully; racing horses for Mr. Turnbull; and hunting and fishing helped fill the idle hours.

Rosedown endured some lean years with the advent of the Civil War, but it remained in the family possession until 1955, when it was purchased by Mr. and Mrs. Milton Underwood. Completely restored, the house and gardens stand today much as they were a century ago, a beautiful picture of a way of life in another era.

THE COTTAGE

Off U. S. Highway 61
Six miles north of St. Francisville
Open daily—Fee

DEVELOPED as a country retreat to escape the heat, mud, fevers, and intense business and social life of bustling New Orleans, the Cottage is a comfortable, low, rambling house. The initial structure, situated on a parcel of land obtained through a grant from the Spanish Crown, dates from 1795.

Figure 13 The Cottage

In 1811, Judge Thomas Butler purchased the modest colonial home and commenced to enlarge the plantation as the need arose. By the time the last addition was made in 1850, the Cottage consisted of twenty rooms, including four upstairs bedrooms, each with a separate sitting room.

Of interest to the visitor is the unusually wide front gallery extending across the front of the house. Blinds, designed to hook from the inside with downward louvers to maintain some privacy from inquisitive Houma and Tunica Indians, are still evident. Important, too, are the antebellum out-buildings surrounding the house, perhaps the most complete grouping in the Parish.

Though used primarily as a summer retreat, the Cottage was no less renowned than their other Feliciana neighbors for its hospitality. The local newspaper claims the Cottage's walls "must have been made of elastic since they never failed to stretch to admit a guest." This lavish praise was put to the test, when Andrew Jackson and his entourage, returning from their victory at Chalmette in 1812, stopped off at the Cottage for a visit. All guests were graciously received and entertained, and in order to accommodate the large group, the host and hostess slept in the pantry.

Correct and proper entertaining was a way of life, and all members of the family were required to help. According to Louise Butler's description, guests usually arrived in their family coach, whereupon the ladies would be taken to the company room to remove their bonnets and pelisses (coats). A quick look in the Psyche, a touch of pomatum for any unruly curls and the ladies were ready to adjourn to the parlor. Cordial, maraschino, or curacao with fruitcake were served, over which the ladies exchanged bits of gossip. Meanwhile, different members of the family took turns supervising the servants in the kitchen. Mamie might need help beating egg whites with switches for floating island, while Eola Mae was busy searing the Spanish cream with a red hot salamander. The gentlemen's return from inspecting the crops was announced, whereupon a huge silver salver filled with crystal goblets surrounding the blossom-filled julep bowl was sent in for their enjoyment. Dinner followed with the proper wine to complement each course. Coffee was served to the well-fed guest in tiny cups, often of old Chelsea or Sèvres, with lumps of loaf sugar placed in a silver dish. For those who desired, stronger spirits could be added. After supper, dancing to stimulate the drowsy and later more coffee and gumbo for any guests in need of further nourishment before retiring. A stay at the Cottage was a memorable event for any guest, and the tradition of hospitality remains even today.

PARLANGE

On Louisiana Highway 1, just off junction with Louisiana Highway 78,
Five miles south of New Roads
Open daily—Fee
Children not admitted

IMAGINE the obstacles to wresting a plantation empire out of the Louisiana wilderness in 1750! Conditions were favorable for Marquis Vincent de Ternant, an energetic French aristocrat, to establish Parlange Plantation. Safe from perilous floods and protected by the military post of Saint Coupée, the selection of the beautiful False River location was propitious.

Entered through an avenue of large oaks and cedars, Parlange is a fine example of early French colonial construction. The first floor of this raised cottage was built of plantation-made brick and was used for storage, smoke rooms, wine cellars and the like. The upper story, escaping the dampness of the land, served as the living quarters for the family and was built of bousillage.

Interesting to note are the four galleries surrounding the house. The line of colonnettes are not in conformation with the doors, and the front entrance is decidedly off center. Then, too, the moldings and ceiling medallions are hand-carved wood instead of the usual plaster they so closely resemble. The heavy wood bars on the ground windows and the more delicate iron bars on the second floor, reflect the frontier era when the house was built.

Upon the marquis's death, his son, Claude Vincent de Ternant, assumed the management of the plantation, its 200 slaves and 10,000 acres. Claude married his ward, Virginie Trahan, who was destined to become Parlange's most colorful mistress.

In five years, she gave Claude four children. Her maternal duty fulfilled, she and Claude commenced traveling back and forth to Paris, where she conducted her salon. Claude died in 1842, and several years later, Virginie married Colonel Charles Parlange, a dashing young man in the French army. A series of tragedies interrupted Virginie's carefree life. First, Henri, Ternant's child, drowned. The placid and always obedient Julie, pushed into

Figure 14 Parlange

an unwanted marriage, died in madness. Colonel Parlange died, but Virginie's most crushing blow was the loss of the handsome young marquis, Marius, the *bon vivant* of the family as well as Virginie's favorite.

Virginie's remaining hope was ten-year-old Charles, her son by Colonel Parlange and from whom the plantation would take its name. When the Civil War erupted, in a desperate attempt to preserve something for her child, Virginie hid her valuables and went forth to meet the Union and Confederate armies alike. Entertaining first General Banks of the Union Army and shortly thereafter General Richard Taylor of the Confederates, she managed to keep Parlange safe and intact for her son. Charles lived up to Virginie's hopes, eventually becoming the lieutenant governor of the state and later a justice of the Louisiana Supreme Court. Even today Virginie is fondly remembered. Descendants recall Alzea, an old family servant, who was buried as she requested, in *la vieille Madame's* black silk petticoat.

Visit Parlange and you will see it much as it was in Virginie's day. Virginie's portrait is there, seeming as Virginie, herself, a little larger than life. Portraits of the children, Virginie's ornate Louis XIV and Empire furniture, the original brick molds used to build Parlange, and family records, help make Parlange a museum in miniature. As such, it has been declared a National Historic Landmark. The present owners, Mr. and Mrs. Walter Parlange are the eighth generation and they, along with Mrs. Parlange, Sr., help receive visitors and continue to maintain the hospitality for which Virginie was so well noted.

MADEWOOD

On Louisiana Highway 308, facing Bayou Lafourche
Near Napoleonville
Open daily—Fee

INSPIRED by author John Darby's vivid description of Bayou Lafourche's rich alluvial soil, the three Pugh brothers from Virginia and Carolina bought small farms along the bayou and then enlarged them with each successful cane harvest. By 1860 the prolific Pugh fortune had grown to two thousand slaves and eighteen plantations valued at more than three million dollars. The patriarch of the Pugh family was Augustin, a quiet and hardhearted fellow who kept his nose in the planters book thinking of ways to increase his harvest. He refused to build a home equal to his fortune and would not even allow his wife the satisfaction of adding a row of columns across the front of their small frame home. He scoffed at his brothers ostentatious life style but remained their astute partner in business.

Thomas Pugh's home, Madewood, is the only plantation left standing of the original three Pugh brothers' homes. While visiting his brother's family at Woodlawn during the 1830s, Thomas decided to settle and build his own home on the bayou, with the intention of outdoing his relatives. Apparently Thomas was anxious to move to Louisiana because he had just been "excused" from the University of North Carolina for his participation in a student clash with the faculty. Once established on the bayou, he met and married Eliza Foley and they reared five sons. Though he died before his home was finished, his wife Eliza supervised its completion.

Madewood was designed by Henry Howard, the architect of Nottoway Plantation, and built between 1840 and 1848 with wood obtained from the plantation acreage; hence the name Madewood. It was intended to resemble a Greek temple with Ionic columns rising from a continuous base or stylobate skyward to a triangular pediment adorned with a Palladian fan window. Across the upstairs gallery runs a diamond design railing and to complete the façade, two side wings echo the predominant elements of the main house. Interior and exterior walls are 18 to 24 inches thick with stucco or plaster over brick. The woodwork throughout the home is finished in *faux bois* and signed by the artist, Cornelius Hennessey.

The spacious and airy rooms on the first floor all open onto a central hallway. Of special interest on the first floor is the ballroom. Weekly balls were a popular source of amusement. With five eligible sons, Eliza Pugh probably kept her ballroom full of fiddlers, fair maidens in hoopskirts, dashing young fellows, and plenty of fine food. Many who came for an evening's entertainment stayed all night. Family members were welcome as long as they wished to stay, and many stayed weeks or months. Every meal became a feast, and with over 250 slaves at Madewood, Miss Eliza had plenty of help to plan and cook the meals. The original ground-level kitchen was placed to the rear of the home for reasons of fire protection. Today it contains antique kitchen equipment collected by the present owner, Mrs. Harold E. Marshall.

On the second floor are four spacious bedrooms with dressing rooms and walk-in closets, a first among the bayou plantations. An outside stairway

Figure 15 Madewood

leads up from the second floor to an enormous attic where huge hand-cut cypress structural beams are visible.

Beyond the home, an iron grillwork fence and the somber shade of age old oaks surround the family burial grounds where marked tombstones herald the final resting place of the Pugh dynasty.

EDWARD DOUGLASS WHITE STATE PARK AND MUSEUM

On Louisiana Highway 1,
About 6 miles North of Thibodaux
Open daily, except Monday—Fee

THE EDWARD DOUGLASS WHITE STATE PARK AND MUSEUM consists of lovely park grounds surrounded by fields of sugar cane. A modest plantation house, built in 1790, constitutes the museum. The Edward Douglass White family were among the first Americans to settle in Lafourche Parish, where, in the early 1800s, small farms and plantations lined both sides of Bayou Lafourche for miles. The architecture of these houses was simple but sturdy, with heavy cypress timbers providing the strength and front galleries the adornment. By the 1830s, the people began to recognize sugar as a great potential paying crop and turning their backs on cotton, they erected large sugar mills on their plantations. As fortunes accrued, successful cane planters replaced their modest homes with mansions on a grander scale.

Edward Douglass White, born in Tennessee, was governor of Louisiana from 1835 to 1839. He operated a sugar plantation on his property on Bayou Lafourche. Besides the dwelling house, there were on this land, outbuildings such as a hospital, slave cabins, and quarters for the cattle, horses, and mules. The hospitals were particularly indispensable in the years 1849–53 when the dreaded cholera and yellow fever were so prevalent in Lafourche Parish.

Governor White married Sidney Ringgold, and fathered four children. The youngest, Edward D. White, Jr., was born on the White plantation in 1844, and became the only Louisiana jurist to serve as Chief Justice of the United States Supreme Court. The senior White died in 1847 of injuries sustained in a steamboat explosion some years earlier. In 1851 the widow White married a French Canadian, André Brousseau, who resided in New Orleans. The administration of the plantation was handled by overseers, but for several years Mrs. Brousseau took a hand in managing the estate. There are records of her purchases, on Magazine Street in New Orleans, of saddles

Figure 16 Edward Douglass White State Park and Museum

and other hardware plus bills for other household goods such as madeira wine (at $1.80 for six bottles) and gumbo. She was among the clientele of Madame Fremineau's Fancy Bonnet store on Canal Street. Little did she know, as she strolled the French Quarter in search of long whalebones, round combs, and kid gloves, that one day there would be erected on Royal Street in front of the Court House a statue of her famous son, just blocks from the shops where she purchased her fancy shawls and French blankets.

The Edward Douglass White House is an example of the earliest type of Louisiana plantation—a raised cottage, constructed by slave labor of hand-hewn cypress put together with wooden pegs and elevated on brick pillars. The house is presently furnished in the 1830–90 period, and among the interesting pieces is a large armoire, part of the dowry brought to Louisiana by the sixteen-year-old bride of the elder White. There are also two quite narrow beds said to have been used as "labor" beds and which must have encouraged a quick delivery. A small serving kitchen is attached to the house and here are found some old cooking utensils and a large sugar bin. The basement, which at one time housed slaves, now has cypress display cases containing various documents pertaining to the White family.

It is difficult to imagine that sleepy Bayou Lafourche was once a main transportation artery connected to the Mississippi River. An excursion to pirogue races held in conjunction with local festivals, followed by a family picnic at Edward Douglass White House can momentarily recapture a simpler, though vigorous, way of life.

MAGNOLIA

On Louisiana Highway 311,
About 3 miles south of Schriever
Open by appointment—Fee

TRADITIONS of rural society, romance, and mystique associated with the Bayou Lafourche region linger in Magnolia Plantation. The Richard Gaillard Ellis family, early émigrés from Virginia, acquired the plantation lands in the 1830s. The modified Greek Revival style of the home indicates it was probably built in 1858, by Ellis' son, Thomas, although family accounts differ. It is easy to imagine clattering carriages conveying guests and family members between Magnolia and Evergreen, the original Ellis plantation.

At Magnolia, organization of columns, doors, and windows is pleasingly symmetrical, and visual interest is heightened by dissimilar patterns of upper and lower ballustrades. The home was constructed of Louisiana cypress, joined with wooden pegs, and the front walls were stuccoed and scored to suggest stone work.

The Ellis family figured prominently in the Civil War. Eliza Ellis, Thomas' sister, married General Braxton Bragg of the Confederate Army. She was an intelligent, poised lady of independent spirit. Their correspondence in the war years indicates that occasionally Bragg followed her advice on military affairs.

The Civil War left its scar on Magnolia. Federal troops destroyed most of the European furnishings when they converted it to a troop hospital. Even the piano was demolished after the soldiers used it as a trough for feeding horses.

After the war, Magnolia Plantation, like many others throughout the South, was offered for sale. Years later, in 1877, Captain John Jackson Shaffer purchased the home. He and his descendants have beautifully restored it. The present owner, M. Lee Shaffer, lives in the house with his wife and two small children. After the destruction wrought by Hurricane Betsy, in 1965, they too, have had to do major renovation work on Magnolia.

Several features of this plantation are of particular interest. The curved

French rosewood staircase leading to the second floor was originally designed for Ducros, a nearby plantation. When the staircase arrived, Ducros was barely under construction, so the builder installed the staircase at Magnolia. In the wall at the back of the staircase, is a curved door, a very rare piece of architectural design. The milkhouse, which is still intact, had an underground stream that ran beneath it to cool the milk.

On the rear porch of Magnolia, hang the original set of slave bells, used to summon each house slave. These bells were serviced every year by the bellman, a traveling repairman of yesteryear. He was one of many merchants who paddled the bayous offering merchandise and service to residents of the area. These *marchands-charrettes* as they were known to the small Cajun farmers, carried news from the city as well as gossip from up the bayou. They loaded their boats with stocks of corn, bacon, ham, dried bison meat, tallow, leather, fur, metal for bullets, and kitchen utensils of every size and variety. Once roads were built, *les marchands* switched to horse-drawn carts to peddle their wares down Bayou Lafourche, known as the "longest street in the world."

Figure 17 Magnolia

OAK ALLEY

On River Road (West Bank) Louisiana Highway 18,
About 2½ miles above Vacherie
Open daily—Fee

TWENTY-EIGHT majestic live oaks flank the entrance way to Oak Alley Plantation. Their topmost leafy branches converge, forming an airy, sun-dappled tunnel through which the visitor is drawn, rewarded at the end by perhaps the most breathtaking view of a Louisiana plantation home. The pale pink structure, centered in its frame of oaks, responds to each change of light and season.

Located sixty miles above New Orleans on the west bank of the meandering Mississippi, Oak Alley, or Bon Séjour, as it was dubbed originally, was built in 1837 by wealthy Jacques Telephere Roman III. Jacques's brother, André, was governor of Louisiana and his sister, Josephine, married the illustrious and inventive Valcour Aimé. Jacques had no desire to compete with his socially prominent relatives, as his interests lay in hunting, fishing, and developing his sugar cane fields. His wife, Josephine Pilié, had more grandiose ideas. She desired a home to rival the beauty of the alley of oaks planted 150 years earlier by a French pioneer. Following architectural renderings which were probably prepared by her father, she commissioned George Swainey to direct the construction of the plantation.

The home, a fine example of Louisiana's Greek Revival architecture, rises two stories high with a hipped roof and perfectly proportioned Doric columns. The Roman family chose to echo the number of oaks with an equal number of columns and slave quarters. The interior was simple but elegant, with four rooms on each floor opening onto a central hallway. Atop the plantation a white-railed belvedere provided a place for Monsieur Roman to survey his land, the river, and the outbuildings, which are no longer in existence.

Until recently, Oak Alley has produced large quantities of cane, fruit, vegetables, cattle, poultry, timber, and pecans. The first scientific cultivation

Figure 18 Oak Alley

of pecans in Louisiana and perhaps in the world was conducted by Antoine, a slave gardener of the Romans', who grafted sixteen trees to obtain a choice variety. These pecans were served annually at family sugarhouse parties held just after grinding season. Each guest dipped a string of the pecans in *cuite*, the thick sugar-cane syrup, while the servants passed a well-fortified punch to the men and eau sucré to the ladies.

The nearby home of Jacques Roman's brother-in-law, Valcour Aimé was also a hub of family and social gatherings. Legend has it that Louis Philippe of France was entertained at a banquet where five-dollar bills were used as cigarette lighters. On another occasion, Aimé bet a visiting dignitary $10,000 that he could serve delicious cuisine with foods grown on his own land. He won his bet but graciously refused to accept the money. The Aimé gardens were some of the finest in America.

The 1860s brought an end to this age of elegant entertaining. Today Oak Alley stands as the only survivor of the Roman family life style. Felicity and St. Joseph plantations, homes of Roman nieces (Valcour Aimé's daughters) are privately owned. The fabulous Valcour Aimé Plantation deteriorated with the decline in family fortune, and was finally destroyed by fire. Oak Alley remains a dramatic memorial to the vision of Josephine and Jacques Roman, preserved with integrity by the present owner, Mrs. Andrew Stewart.

ALBANIA PLANTATION

On Louisiana Highway 182 (old U. S. Highway 90)
About 1 mile east of Jeanerette—Open daily—Fee

ALBANIA PLANTATION mansion is almost hidden from the highway by the large oaks. Upon entering the drive, one is struck by the beauty of the rear façade, and marvels at the ingenuity of the architects who created an imposing view for those guests arriving by horse and carriage, and an equally lovely bayou façade, which welcomed guests coming down the Teche by boat. The rear façade of the house has upper and lower galleries enclosed with balustrades and supported by six square columns which reach to the gabled roof. The bayou side has two extended smaller galleries on both levels supported by four columns.

Records indicate that the property was part of two land grants received by Charles François Grevemberg, a captain in the French army, from Louis XVI and from Napoleon I.

The house was constructed in the late 1830s out of cypress brought in by boat from the swamps, and it remained in the Grevemberg family until 1885, when it was purchased by Delgado and Co. at foreclosure proceedings. Isaac Delgado maintained it until 1910, when it was bequeathed to the city of New Orleans for the maintenance of the Delgado Trade School and the Delgado Museum. In 1957, the home was bought at public auction by Mr. and Mrs. James H. Bridges. It is believed that the plantation was among the first Louisiana sugar-producing plantations, and its sugar mill has operated for over one hundred years.

The floor plan of the home was most conducive to the elegant entertainment of friends. Two large parlors dominate the lower level, one of which opens onto the rear gallery by means of windows, with unique small-door openings at the bottom. This design facilitates use either as windows or entrances to the gallery. It is said that John James Audubon was among the visitors to Albania, and that he roamed the bayou and nearby swamps in search of egrets and pelicans to add to his other famous sketches of Louisiana wildlife.

Figure 19 Albania Plantation

Tales of lavish parties abound, and for these occasions not only did many guests arrive by boat from New Orleans, but also transported down the bayou were orchestras, delicacies, wines, and French pastries. One dinner menu, said to date from the 1840s, included such opulent fare as quail on toast, roast turkey with cornbread dressing, daube glacée, quince jelly, and soufflé potatoes, accompanied no doubt by a fine French burgundy wine.

The interior of the mansion has been preserved in a manner befitting a gracious antebellum home. Among the furnishings are many eighteenth-century antique pieces of mahogany, walnut, rosewood, and cherry. Particularly reminiscent of bygone days are the large plantation beds draped with French lace mosquito netting. And, among the paintings, there is one of the bayou side of the house by Adrien Persac, an artist who captured the beauty of many homes of this era. One of the many dressing rooms contains a collection of dresses and accessories dating from the Civil War. And of special interest to little girls and collectors is a fabulous collection of about a thousand antique dolls. Would that the dolls could speak to us of their lives in such fairytale surroundings as these old plantation homes.

SHADOWS-ON-THE-TECHE

On Main Street in New Iberia
Open daily—Fee

IT WOULD BE ideal if visitors could approach the Shadows-on-the-Teche plantation by pirogue or flat boat via Bayou Teche. Such a first glimpse of this romantic red brick house, surrounded by moss-draped oaks, willows, cypress, and magnolia trees would create the immediate illusion of a past era that it embodies. As it is, one must enter the grounds from the Main Street of New Iberia, which only temporarily delays your passage into bygone days.

The Shadows was built by a wealthy sugar planter, David Weeks, in the early 1830s, and occupied by his descendants until it was bequeathed by Weeks Hall in 1958 to the National Trust for Historic Preservation. The National Trust chose to restore it to its antebellum glory with the assistance of some 2,000,000 invaluable documents and letters carefully saved in the house.

David Weeks had handled the property for his father, an Englishman who received the land grant from the Spanish. Unfortunately, he did not live to enjoy the town house that he had spent years planning and constructing, as he died while on a business trip to Connecticut. But his widow, the former Mary Conrad, shared her husband's enthusiasm for the superbly designed house and especially for the gardens that she had planned herself, and she was determined to stay there with her children. Thus she handled the plantation affairs until her remarriage in 1841 to Judge John Moore, a Virginia-born lawyer. Together they enjoyed the lively and largely family-oriented life. There are many references in family letters to visits up and down the Teche and their sharing of the bounty from the vegetable gardens and the fruit trees. And what a bounty it was! —artichokes, cauliflowers, cabbage, peppers, squash, many varieties of peas and beans, eggplant, mirlitons, and innumerable salad greens. The Weeks ladies derived much pleasure from gardening and exchanging seeds, cuttings, and shrubs, and

Figure 20 Shadows-on-the-Teche

they always mentioned in their letters the effects of the weather on their crops and their blossoms. These ladies likewise exchanged recipes, and among the favorites were those for fowl and game abundant in the area—quail, venison, and duck. There will no doubt be many studies made from the vast archive of Shadows material that will cast light on the social and cultural history of the families who have lived there.

The architecture of the mansion blends Greek Revival style with Virginia influences and combines fine design with functional Louisiana adaptations. The street side has classic columns rising from the ground to the simple entablature which supports the roof. There are upper and lower galleries and shutter-enclosed stairs. The bayou side of the house has a recessed gallery with brick arches below and turned Doric columns above. The interior is a characteristic plan of three rooms across, two deep, with no hallway. The interior woodwork is notable in its detail as are the plaster cornices. All of the furniture dates from before 1865 and much of the furnishings, including fine paintings and silver, have been handed down by generations of the Weeks family. The entire collection is now restricted to family artifacts.

There are presently archaeological excavations in progress on the Shadows property and the foundation of early slave quarters have been found. How fortunate that this Louisiana plantation will continue to live because of the generosity of its last owner, who insured its future.

ACADIAN HOUSE MUSEUM

Off Louisiana Highway 31,
In St. Martinville
Open daily—Fee

ONE TENDS to enter Evangeline State Park in St. Martinville reflecting on the poetry of this region immortalized by Longfellow. The Acadian House Museum is located in the oak-filled park, its setting enhanced by an exquisite rear garden. This land is truly rich in legend. Originally the home of the Attakapas Indians, it was subsequently inhabited by the French recipients of land grants who began arriving about 1755. The Acadians followed, driven from Nova Scotia in the 1760s, and by the late eighteenth century, refugees from the French Revolution were settling the area. Popular local stories run the gamut of tales of the cannibal tribes to histories of the flight of the French Acadians or "Cajuns" to Louisiana, and finally the accounts of the grand world of "le petit Paris," as the area was known during the years of the gay social life of the emigrant French aristocracy.

The Acadian House Museum is situated on land which was originally the estate of a Frenchman named D'Hauterive who migrated from France in the 1760s. A home site was established here by Chevalier Paul Augustin le Pelletier de la Houssaye around 1763.

The structure of the house represents the sturdy construction work of the Acadian farmer who found locally all the components necessary for a comfortable dwelling place. The swamps provided cypress trees which were usually felled by slaves, and the wood utilized in the interior and exterior of the dwelling. This wood was ideal as it withstood both the elements and insects. The walls of the ground floor are made of bricks, which were traditionally molded and baked on the premises, and the upper-story walls are a combination of soil and moss mixed to a mortar.

The house is two rooms wide and one-and-a-half rooms deep. On the ground floor is found the dining room and a bedroom which might have served as a sick or recovery room. The staircase is typically on the exterior and the second-floor bedrooms open directly into one another.

Figure 21 Acadian House Museum

The resourcefulness of the early settlers is likewise evidenced by the furnishings exhibited here. The cypress tree seems to have been indispensable to daily life as it yielded the timbers from which were fashioned not only the roof, walls, and pegs to fasten all together, but also the beds, chairs, religious shrines, the prie-dieu, or kneeling bench, the weasels for weaving cotton, and the pestles for grinding the rice or corn. Equally interesting are the artifacts exhibited in the reconstructed kitchen house which recall meals prepared from ample local provisions—fish from the nearby bayou, game from the woods, and corn, rice and vegetables from the fertile fields.

Naturally, a must for any romanticist is a visit to the centuries-old Gabriel Oak near the house and the Evangeline Oak farther down the road on the banks of Bayou Teche, both capable of stirring the imagination to dreams of yesteryear.

LOYD HALL

Off U. S. Highway 71,
Near Cheneyville
Open daily except Tuesday—Fee

FIELDS OF SOYBEANS and cotton, intersected by quiet country roads and tiny bayous, provide the setting for Loyd Hall—an imposing dark brick mansion, rich in legend and history. The house is located south of Alexandria, near the small town of Cheneyville, Louisiana.

The three-storied plantation house has matching galleries across the front and rear. The architectural style is more comparable to homes found in the New Orleans Garden District, such as the Payne Strachan House, than that of rural Louisiana plantations.

A broad hall runs through the center of all three floors, with four large corner rooms on the first two, measuring twenty by twenty with eighteen-foot ceilings. The plaster work on these ceilings is glorious, ornate, and in excellent condition. Each room's medallion has its own design and was made by pouring plaster into a mold, then attaching it to the ceiling with glue.

There is, unfortunately, little or no documented history concerning Loyd Hall, partially because there have been so many different owners (perhaps twenty) and partially because the Union Army burned Alexandria, thus destroying all public records. However, from what historians and researchers can reconstruct, and there are many conflicting opinions, a William Loyd from London built the house in 1816. His name was originally spelled with two L's, but since he was considered a "black sheep," he was required by his family to drop one "L."

William was hanged on his own property in 1864 by Union soldiers for aiding the Confederate Army, and Union soldiers stayed at Loyd Hall for three nights in May 1864 before the burning of Alexandria. James, William's son, who was twelve years old when the house was built, was also killed during the Civil War in 1864.

In 1850, James Loyd had placed a mortgage on the plantation and upon his death, Jasper Sharrith was sent to oversee the mortgaged plantation.

Figure 22 Loyd Hall

Sharrith lived there from 1864 to 1876. Sharrith and General Sherman were close friends and neighbors in Ohio, and Sherman stayed at Loyd Hall in 1876. Mrs. James Loyd died in 1870 and the mortgage was foreclosed. The plantation was sold for the first of many times.

There are many mysteries and stories associated with the house. Two bullets in the wall of the front hall and Indian arrowheads in the door to the dining room are without explanation. There is a grave in the cellar which might be that of Inez Loyd, James's sister, who committed suicide when she was rejected by her lover, or it could belong to a soldier whom Mrs. William Loyd is said to have shot on the third floor. A bullet hole and blood stains on the floor give testimony to this tale. Legend has it that a ghost appears on the third floor balcony at midnight, playing a violin, mourning the death of either Inez or the soldier.

An interesting feature to the rear of the house is the way station. Stagecoaches often stopped at Loyd Hall in order to provide travelers and horses with refreshment and a brief rest. Many interesting kitchen implements, simple furnishings, and the large fireplace can be inspected by the visitor. Travelers using Bayou Boeuf, which flows well in front of Loyd Hall, probably took advantage of the way station, and a chance to gather news of happenings along the bayous.

Today the plantation is owned by Mrs. Virginia Fitzgerald, who lives at Loyd Hall with her son and his family. The house is in extremely good condition and has had no major renovation except the addition of plumbing. The plantation is a working one, whose present acreage is 640. Original crops included indigo and cotton, and today it is soybeans and some cotton.

TANTE HUPPÉ PRUD'HOMME HOUSE

At 424 Jefferson Street in Natchitoches
Open by appointment and during the Annual Historic Tour of Natchitoches—Fee

THE NATCHITOCHES or Cane River area enjoys a special introduction, aptly provided by a visit to the Roque House, situated at the entrance of Front Street at the river in the town of Natchitoches. The building, used as a museum of local history, was originally located on the Cane River at Isle Brevelle and is one of the only pure French colonial dwellings left in the state. It is owned by Museum Contents, Inc. and is open during the summer months and for all Natchitoches tours. Here one may obtain brochures, maps, and other information on the region.

In the center of Natchitoches, at 424 Jefferson Street, stands the Tante Huppé House. It was built in 1827 by Antoine Prud'homme, a wealthy cotton planter, for his daughter, Susette. Susette's first husband was Dr. Bernard Lafon, one of the earliest Louisiana doctors. After Lafon's death, Susette married Andrew LeCompte, a famous breeder of race horses, and finally, a third husband, Jean Baptiste Huppé. Huppé died in 1836, and the following year Susette's only son died. Although her life was marked by the loss of loved ones, Susette "Tante Huppé" lived to become one of the legends of the area, opening her town house constantly for friends and family.

Susette Huppé died in 1861. Records show that Phanon Prud'homme of Oakland Plantation bought the home in 1858. Oakland Plantation, the Prud'homme house, was thirteen miles from Natchitoches where the Prud'homme girls were studying in a convent. The family used Tante Huppé's house as a town house to facilitate visiting the children. The house remained in the Prud'homme family until 1969, when it was purchased by the Robert DeBlieuxs.

The house is rare in that it contains its original light fixtures, curtain rods, window panes, hardware, and even some paint. Viewed from the street, the one-and-a-half-story house seems smaller than it is. A symmetrical Greek Revival façade reveals the central hall floor plan typical of the early 1800s.

Walls are constructed of hand-hewn cypress sills and posts filled between with brick, then completely faced with brick on the exterior. An artist was hired to stencil white mortar lines on top of red oxide paint, covering the bricks to represent bricks an inch thicker than those actually used.

There are eighteen rooms in the house, nine fire places, and eleven outside doors, one in each ground-floor room. All of the latches and keys on the doors and windows are original. All doors are cypress but were painted to represent a grainier wood. This paint is still on the doors. The floors are the original one-and-a-half-inch-thick red pine and are naturally finished.

Across the back of the house is a ground level porch from which extends an old brick patio recently unearthed when Mr. DeBlieux was digging a garden.

The two-story servants' quarters and kitchen are connected to the rear of the house. They are of stone, brick, and cypress, and have a gallery across the second floor.

With few exceptions, all furniture in the house is from Natchitoches

Figure 23 Tante Huppé Prud'homme House

Parish. In the hall is a table owned by Tante Huppé. A piece in the dining room is an original Duncan Phyfe sideboard which came to Natchitoches in 1815. The bedrooms all contain handsome armoires and beds—one of very fine French mahogany made for Madame Ben Metoyer, a free person of color, prominent in the history of the region, in 1835.

The library houses an extensive collection of old books representing over a hundred Natchitoches families. Nearly all are signed and dated. Among those found in the house were medical books which belonged to Dr. Lafon, Bernardine's books, and Susette's own cookbook, which is written in French, as were most of the books and letters. One of the oldest books in the collection is a rare 1734 edition of *Histoire des Plantes Vénéneuses et Suspectes.*

When the Phanon Prud'hommes used the house as their town house, the library was Julie's room. Displayed on a mahogany Empire table is a songbook opened to "Dixie Land." This copy of the song is dedicated to Julie and it predates by several years what was thought to be the oldest published version of "Dixie." The tune is the same but the words are different from the contemporary version.

The DeBlieuxs' knowledge and interest in Natchitoches history, their excellent taste, and commitment to regional preservation efforts heighten the historic and architectural importance of the home.

OAKLAND

On Louisiana Highway 119, at Bermuda
Midway between Derry and Natchitoches
Open by appointment and for the Annual Historic Tour of Natchitoches—Fee

FRAMED by giant oak trees, facing the Cane River, stands Oakland. It belongs to the J. Alphonse Prud'hommes, the eighth generation living on the same site. The site is a part of a land grant from Louis XV given in the eighteenth century to Dr. Jean Baptiste Prud'homme—Docteur du Roi.

Oakland is the second house to be built on this property. The first was an early French type and was set much closer to the river. Pierre Prud'homme, eldest son of Dr. Prud'homme, started Oakland in 1818 and completed it in 1821. It was built in the usual Creole style, of heart cypress, joined with wooden pegs. Walls of the foundation, enclosing a ground level cellar, are of brick and adobe mixed with deer hair. The oak trees, imported from the Mississippi Gulf coast, and the formal garden in front of the house were planted five years later. Some ancient boxwood is still growing in the garden. The garden is outlined with many wine and ale bottles of fine old vintage that were imported from France, along with fine fruits for making cordials, cherry bounce, and peach brandy. The bottles are laid bottom side up, a design used in rural France in the wine sections. The house and gardens are enclosed by the white wooden picket fence.

There was a year-round gallery on all sides of the house. A portion of the rear one has been enclosed to make a modern kitchen and breakfast room. Slender octagonal columns support the roof.

In 1821, before the house was completed, the Prud'hommes went to France to buy furniture, and upon their return found it necessary to enlarge the house, particularly the dining room as they had bought an enormous dining table and many chairs. It was well that they did, for Oakland in succeeding generations was the scene for huge family dinners which featured such delicacies as coon gumbo, blackbirds, venison, squab, and blood pudding.

Although much of the furniture was brought from Paris, there are some

Figure 24 Oakland

interesting pieces made on the plantation. All latches, bolts, and hinges were made on the plantation, but the brass knobs were from Paris. A treasure of leather-bound books, all in French, published in Paris in the eighteenth and nineteenth centuries, have remained with the family along with many old records and manuscripts. A stranger's room where itinerant salesmen and artists stayed overnight was a typical room in many of the plantations and had entrance ways only from the gallery.

In the basement a small museum has been arranged including old kitchen equipment, doctors' instruments, grave markers, and the earliest drilling tools in America, fashioned on the plantation by a talented slave. Gas was discovered at Oakland before the first well was drilled in Pennsylvania. The original basement had a room where the mammy or nurse lived directly below the master bedroom, with stairs and a trap door entering into it.

At one time, a detached kitchen which had a covered walkway, lead to the house. It also had a smokehouse where bacon, venison, hams, and other meats were smoked with wood from chestnut trees. Pigeonnières supplied squab for pigeon pie.

The most interesting outbuilding is the old carpenter shop, now a country store. This is the shop where all of the work in building the main house was done. It is to the left of the house and worth a visit.

Oakland is most interesting because of the continuous family ownership, memorabilia, and original pieces preserved from its past. A visit to the area should also include a drive farther south on Highway 484, past Melrose Plantation, the house of primitive artist Clementine Hunter, and the beautiful and unspoiled serenity of the Cane River, and the surrounding countryside.

BEAU FORT

On Louisiana Highway 494
About 10 miles south of Natchitoches
Open for Annual Historic Tour of Natchitoches in October—Fee

A GREAT PART of the charm of the Natchitoches region belongs to the plantations south of the city along the Cane River. Following a winding road, one arrives at Beau Fort, a house and property in pristine condition. Its general atmosphere is one of serenity and simplicity.

Here, as at the Tante Huppé House, the name Prud'homme appears. Jean Baptiste Prud'homme arrived in 1759 as the fourth Royal Military Surgeon of the King to be assigned to Natchitoches. One old record shows that he bought an arpent of land from the estate of the late Madame de St. Denis on December 29, 1759. This no doubt was added to the land grant given the Prud'hommes by King Louis XV of France in 1764. The land ran along both sides of the Cane River, Old Red River, from the town of Natchitoches to Cloutierville. Jean Baptiste Prud'homme built a small two- or three-room house on the river bank near the present site of Oakland Plantation house. This small house was typical of the times and was similar to the Roque House in Natchitoches.

Prud'homme married twice and had six children. The eldest son, Pierre Emanuel Prud'homme, inherited the land of his surgeon-coroner-planter father. In 1818, Pierre began the house that still stands at Oakland. In 1830, he built Beau Fort for his second son, Louis Narcisse Prud'homme, on the site of one of the original five forts of Natchitoches, Fort Prud'homme. This house was handed down in the family until 1937, when the late husband of the present owner, Mrs. C. Vernon Cloutier, purchased it along with its 313 acres of land. Mr. Cloutier was a descendant of the Cloutiers of Cloutierville and she is a direct descendant of a daughter of Dr. Jean Baptiste Prud'homme, who married a Roquier in 1782.

The house is set at the end of an alley of live oak trees planted by the Cloutiers soon after they moved to the plantation as newlyweds, on New Year's Eve 1937. There are five acres of lawn and gardens surrounding the

Figure 25 Beau Fort

house which are watered by two of the original five underground cisterns. The Cloutiers have restored the house and made a few changes. The dining room was enlarged, an inside door was cut to the "stranger's room," and the floor in the room was replaced. A former occupant had a still which burned a hole through the floor. This room is typical of plantation houses of this era and locale and was accessible only from the front gallery. It was used as a guest room for itinerant artists or travelers who needed lodging for the night.

The gallery runs eighty-four feet across the front of the house and also along the left side. The house is two rooms deep. Handsome french doors connect each front room to the gallery. Back rooms open onto a brick patio and lovely formal garden, an addition made by the Cloutiers. The original beautiful cypress floors remain throughout the house. Many of the log rafters are forty feet long. The walls are adobe. The modern kitchen wing was added to the right rear of the house, since the original kitchen had long since burned.

The living room, dining room, and three bedrooms are furnished with antiques, mainly from old homes in the New Orleans area. The punka, a fan suspended from the ceiling and worked manually by a servant, is still over the dining room table. The light fixtures, also from old homes, have been converted to electricity. The mahogany Louisiana sofa, upholstered with the material from a homespun bedspread, and a chair in the library, date from the early 1800s. The French Creole plantation desk is made of rosewood and walnut.

Many fine portraits of Cloutier ancestors hang in the living room. One painted in 1780, is of Mrs. Bossier Buard, and another of her son, Antoine, who were related to the man for whom the city of Bossier, Louisiana was named. A third is of the first Cloutier of the parish. On another wall is a fan of ivory and gold-leaf painted with señoritas in ball gowns and conquistadors in armor. It dates back to the Spanish occupation of Louisiana.

Beau Fort is open for the Natchitoches Historical Tour each October. However, a drive down the historic Cane River for a glimpse at this beautifully maintained home is as great a pleasure for travelers today, as it must have been for the early occupants of the "stranger's room."

MYRTLE HILL

On Louisiana Highway 5,
About 2 miles West off Louisiana Highway 175, at Kingston
Open by appointment and during Holiday in Dixie Tour in Spring—Fee

A HOUSE with a legend of shattered romance, Myrtle Hill is situated near Land's End and Buena Vista. A planter, Edward Riggs, ordered the house to be built in 1853, upon becoming engaged. He chose a site amid rolling hills and running streams in DeSoto Parish. Sparing no effort or expense,

Figure 26 Myrtle Hill

he enlisted the aid of Mrs. W. B. Means, the wife of a neighboring planter, to help select handsome furnishings in New Orleans. His intended changed her mind, however, and Mr. Riggs, unable to face living alone in the bridal house, sold it to James Taylor Means, the son of his neighbor.

Myrtle Hill is a single story clapboard house, the original portion consisting of four large rooms separated by a spacious central hall. The gracious entrance way is a classical four pillared portico. A gallery connects a rear wing which was added by Mr. Means. The floors are random-width heart pine. The wide woodwork and heavy broad doors add elegance to this well-proportioned small home. The front door, fashioned from a single block of wood, is two inches thick, and bears a deep scar inflicted by a Union soldier's bayonet. The closets, an unusual feature for a house of this period, are quite large.

During the early Reconstruction period, a Union scouring party arrested Mr. Means because of his political activities for the cause of the Confederacy. He was taken to Shreveport where he and other Confederate patriots were soon released because the grand jury failed to indict them. Following Reconstruction, Mr. Means was elected to the state legislature.

Two of the original cluster of outbuildings have been preserved. The smokehouse, essential for curing meat, fish, and game, still stands, as well as another small building now used as a garden room. A plantation bell stands on a sixty-five-foot tower behind the house. It was reportedly cast from 65 per cent silver, and its clear sound can be heard for miles.

In 1937, Myrtle Hill was bought by Mr. and Mrs. Ray P. Oden of Shreveport. They have beautifully restored the house and gardens. The furnishings chosen by the Odens are period pieces in excellent taste. A handsomely carved walnut half-canopy bed is the focal point of the master bedroom. It once belonged to General Pierre Beauregard, a famous Confederate general. Complementing the bed is an English mahogany armoire, ten feet in height. The armoire doors are fastened at the top and bottom with pin bolts, a type of hardware that predates the use of hinges.

Surrounded by a grove of approximately two million pines, Myrtle Hill appears to the visitor very much the same as it must have seemed to early callers arriving by horse, carriage, or wagon. This well-loved home is today, as in years past, the scene of many happy family gatherings.

LAND'S END

On Red Bluff, about 3½ miles south of the junction of Linwood Avenue
   and the Stonewall-Frierson Road
Open by appointment and during the DeSoto Parish Historic Tour—Fee

NORTHWEST LOUISIANA was truly the "end of the land" when Henry Marshall selected the site of his plantation in 1835, only fifteen miles from the Texas border. A law graduate of Union College and a colonel on the staff of the governor of South Carolina, he looked to the West for opportunities to exercise his great talents.

Marshall's first home for his family was a large log house, to which they made a remarkably good adjustment. In a letter dated 1844, to her father at the state Senate in New Orleans, Mary Marshall related: "The day before Christmas Eve, the children walked to the bayou and brought home plenty of myrtle and pine to dress the house. Grandmother remarked that a log house is much more convenient than a plastered one, for you can stick the bushes in the cracks instead of having the trouble of putting up nails."

In spite of the frontier character of northern Louisiana, the Marshalls carried with them the life style of their previous home. The library, much of which remains today, reflects orthodox tastes in literature. A diary kept by one of his six daughters tells that in the month of January 1856, she "read Scott's *Talisman* aloud to Grandpa and the children and commenced *The Tales of Grandfather* and Thomson's *Winter*." On the piano she practiced *Norma* and "Musette de Nina." Letters of Marshall's sons show hunting and fishing to be their main diversion. They describe the abundance of wild turkey, deer, rabbit, and dove. In 1844, Mrs. Marshall wrote that "Tom was delighted a few days since of having killed at one shot twelve blackbirds. I made them up into a pie which Tom said he wished that you were here to enjoy with us in eating. The place abounds in the greatest variety of birds that I have ever seen. They run about the yard almost as tamely as the chickens." Vegetables of all kinds, including rice, were grown on the place, while excellent wines and brandies were brought from New Orleans.

Figure 27 Land's End

By 1857, Marshall had built his manor house. It is a two-and-a-half-story structure of Greek Revival design. The six fluted Ionic columns are set on pilastered bases a little out from the edge of the gallery. Foundations are visible at the rear of the house where two one-story wings extended. A two-room detached kitchen, now destroyed, once served the household. A visitor to the house about 1880, remarked that "Land's End looked like a small village, with the numerous out buildings and slave quarters." Much of the furniture is original and in the elegant style of the period.

From this home, Marshall went to Baton Rouge in 1861 as a delegate to the Secession Convention. He also represented his state at Montgomery and Richmond. Marshall was a signer of the Confederate Constitution and was a member of the Confederate Congress. He lost two sons in the War and died in 1864—a year before Appomattox.

Colonel Henry Furman Means, a great-grandson of Marshall, and the present owner of Land's End, is endeavoring to preserve the furnishings, the house, and its place in history.

BUENA VISTA

On Red Bluff Road, about 2½ miles east of U. S. Highway 171
Just past Stonewall
Open by appointment—Fee

IN 1839, Boykin Witherspoon, like other Carolina planters, looked westward in search of fertile, "healthy" country on which to establish his plantation. Since crop rotation was not widely practiced, the Carolina lands were fast becoming depleted, and large slaveowners needed fresh land to continue their vast farming operations. Witherspoon purchased 5,500 acres in DeSoto Parish, but his wife refused to move until a church and a school were established nearby. Like other pioneer families of the region, the Wither-spoons had to endure some hardships in moving to this frontier territory. When the family finally came in 1854, they brought their furniture on a flat boat, which sank en route. Fortunately, most of the cargo was recovered, dried and sent on its way up the river to its destination.

The Witherspoons lived in a log house until their manor house was completed, in 1860, by M. Robbins, a popular architect-builder of the area. Mr. Robbins, who designed Land's End and other DeSoto homes, was able to achieve an uncommonly high standard of craftsmanship, using largely untutored, yet skilled, slave workmen. His trademark was tall columns, set independently on brick pilasters and a little out from the edge of the gallery floor, so that rain did not fall on the floor boards. This construction also afforded maximum shade from the hot summer sun. Buena Vista's eight columns are octagon-shaped, separating the carefully mortised cypress grillwork. The house is two-and-a-half stories tall with four well-propor-tioned rooms on the first and second floors, and two on the third. A large square stairway, unusual for this area, connects the three floors.

Situated on a hill surrounded by great elms and oaks, Buena Vista, as the name implied, is set in the midst of a natural park. It was noted for its pure spring water and "healthy location". On the west side of the house, a gnarled old wisteria vine winds its way to the support of a tall Magnolia tree.

Figure 28 Buena Vista

Like other wealthy planter families of the region, the Witherspoons' life style was quiet and self-contained. They read, played the piano, sewed and wrote letters. Visitors were infrequent and very welcome, especially if they bore interesting news. Mrs. Witherspoon wrote often to her two daughters attending Miss Hull's school in New Orleans. In one letter, she inquired about some gossip she had heard from a recent visitor concerning an admirer of her younger daughter. "He was *charmed* and *refreshed* at having met a bashfull young lady, such a rare thing in these days of *fast* ladies."

Until 1960, Buena Vista remained in the Witherspoon family and operated as a cotton plantation. Its present owner is Dr. Clayton Smith of Shreveport, who has furnished the house with a fine collection of period furniture. In 1968, the Theatre Guild of New York produced the motion picture *The Slaves*, using Buena Vista as its filming location. An upstairs gallery was added to the house and several outbuildings designed in the style of the period were constructed.

WINTER QUARTERS

On Louisiana Highway 604,
About 3 miles Southwest of Newellton
Open daily—Fee

NESTLED on a sloping hill above Lake St. Joseph, Winter Quarters represents three distinct styles of living, and tells much of the personal lives of
its former occupants. Shortly before the Louisiana Purchase was signed in
1803, Job Routh, and Englishman recently settled in Natchez, acquired a
Spanish land grant of 800 acres in Tensas Parish, the last such grant made.
He was industrious and hard-working and soon had acquired great wealth,
planting cotton on his land and increasing acreage as his plantation prospered.

The original structure of Winter Quarters was built as a hunting lodge
for use during the winter season. Local legend tells that the plantation
derived its name from the fact that General U. S. Grant and his Union troops
spent the winter of 1863 at the site. Actually, the house was called Winter
Quarters long before the War. As Job Routh's children began raising families, they too became planters and began building homes all around the lake.
During the winter, each family entertained numerous visiting relatives from
Kentucky, Missouri, Arkansas, and Virginia. Their visits precipitated a long
series of merry revelries. There were dinners, balls, picnics, horse races,
cock fights, and boat races, with crews composed of their slaves. Perhaps,
Job's rustic little hunting lodge was a peaceful retreat from the social whirl-
wind.

Shortly after 1820, Winter Quarters underwent remodeling at the hands
of Ann Routh Ogden, Job's daughter. Five rooms were added and show more
careful construction than the original primitive hunting lodge. The home
was still used as a vacation retreat, since the Ogdens maintained a town
house in Natchez, across the Mississippi River. It was in these five rooms
that the Union troops stayed overnight and planned their campaign on
several occasions during the spring of 1863.

The next family to occupy Winter Quarters was that of Dr. Haller Nutt, a wealthy young planter, who used his scientific knowledge to improve the variety of cotton which he grew on his two plantations, Evergreen and Araby. In 1849, he married Julia Williams, a grandniece of Job Routh, and purchased Winter Quarters as a first home for his wife and family. In enlarging the house, Dr. Nutt expanded the front gallery across the entire house and designed a roof which extended far beyond the gallery so that there was complete shade. The family could sit in comfort on the front porch and watch the boat races on the lake. The large central hall caught the breezes from the rear of the house. This final addition to Winter Quarters is one-and-a-half stories high with large, usable rooms on the upper story. In decorating his home, Dr. Nutt used his own formulas for staining the walls in shades of elderberry, goldenrod, and lavender. The study contains many of Dr. Nutt's prescriptions and instructions useful in running an antebellum plantation.

In the spring of 1863, the Yankees marched along Lake St. Joseph burning and destroying plantations on their way. Winter Quarters was the only home

Figure 29 Winter Quarters

of about fifteen such places which was spared from the torch. Of the numerous original outbuildings, the barn alone escaped destruction by the invading Union troops. The story goes that Mrs. Nutt, eavesdropping through the upstairs floor, overheard the Union officers planning their campaign of destruction. She then made her way from Lake St. Joseph to General Grant's camp at Milliken's Bend. There she offered to feed and quarter his troops if he would promise to spare her home. Perhaps because the Nutts were Union sympathizers, their lovely home was saved and remains today, completely restored and furnished, one of the most interesting and historic homes in Louisiana.

LOUISIANA COOKERY

All recipes are for eight portions,
unless otherwise stated.

JAMBALAYA, crayfish pie and a filé gumbo . . ." a joyous refrain from a bayou ballad—taunting anyone familiar with the exciting flavors of Louisiana's Creole cookery. For along with unforgettable plantation homes, reclining in the recesses of the landscape; food, good food (and, mon dieu, such highly seasoned food!) assures local residents of a continuing source of pride. The people of Louisiana have, with love and joy, preserved and "passed on" the culinary achievements of their unique and multicultured past.

As Louisiana's terrain and cultural background are considerably different in the northern and southern areas, it is not surprising that two types of cookery evolved: the simple, hardy fare of the northern settlements; and the enriched gravy-laden Creole dishes of the southern parishes. New Orleans, culinary capital of the Southland, rates special attention, since her cosmopolitan residents added sophistication and elegance to the preparation and serving of basic Creole meals.

American pioneer life style dominated the culture of upstate Louisiana, and those who settled there necessarily practiced frontier frugality. Rough-hewn farmers often restricted their harvest to a single edible crop, usually corn. This lop-eared plant was a major source of grain, and by its versatility, frequently replaced bread on the table. Sweet dishes, thin coffee, and rather bland seasonings were characteristic of the settler's preferences in food. Culinary taste on the larger plantations, however, more nearly reflected that of the Virginias and Carolinas, from whence the owners had emigrated.

Black-eyed peas were eaten for good luck on New Year's Day, but most festive occasions, such as the Fourth of July, were, and still are celebrated with barbecues. Juicy meats turned on spits and generous helpings of side dishes (Irish potatoes, Virginia spoon breads, corn muffins, and hash) were served from huge vats. Venison and pork were the most oft eaten meats;

yet buffalo, possum, rail and snipe were among the native wildlife that could be hunted year round. A fine selection of fruits and nuts grew in the fertile Red River Valley and the uplander enjoyed a variety of fish and crustaceans from local fresh waterways. "Potlicker" over cornpone was a favorite dish in Caddo Parish and housewives were proficient in the use of dumplings and noodles. Food was never discarded, and leftovers were scraped into the daily soup which continually simmered over the fire, a practice common to all cultures in Louisiana.

"Creole cookery" is a term defined by time and tradition as applying to the cuisine found in the lower parts of Louisiana and perfected in the New Orleans and Teche areas. Recipes handed down through Creole families represent the fusion of European, West Indian, and domestic influences. French colonists brought a wealth of recipes that were to form the basis of Creole cooking. Robust Spanish colonials followed and imposed their own spicy touches to established dishes; the Mexicans later made similar contributions. German immigrants who farmed near the mouth of the river became the largest producers of local rice. Like corn in the uplands, rice was the staple of lowland tables. Italian colonists increased the use of garlic and hot peppers; curries and delicate spices were imported from far off India. Even a few Chinese epicureans made their presence felt.

Louisiana's indigenous inhabitants, the red men, helped enrich budding culinary practices when they generously introduced their European usurpers to hitherto unknown foods. Choctaws and Chickasaws brought the colonists strange herbs; and curious eyes watched these Indians' peculiar ways of preparing corn and game. Yet, popping corn soon became a festive and enduring pastime and Creole ladies eagerly learned the Indians' art of crystallizing fruit. The Choctaws regularly appeared selling a fine powder made from ground sassafras leaves. "Filé" it was dubbed by the Creoles—but the Indians themselves called it "kombo." And here perhaps, is the origin to the name given those rich Creole soups, or "gumbos."

Finally, one must consider the culinary inventiveness of gentle black folk who were imported as slaves from Africa and Santo Domingo. The beloved Negro "Mammy," her head bound in a colorful tignon, could neither read nor write; her authority over the kitchen was second only to the mistress. She cooked with a flair, not a recipe; seasoning to taste, not measurement. Mistress's thrift and Mammy's creativity resulted in a number of marvelous Creole recipes calling for the poorer cuts of meat, chicken necks, ham bones, and fish heads. Mammy was assisted by helpers who chopped garden fresh herbs and seasonings for the daily pot. And like any good black cook of the area, she excelled in preparing succulent local favorites; jambalayas, shrimp Creole, and gumbos, always adding meat and fish stocks or wine to their sauces. Varied as the dishes were, Mammy confidently began most with a good French *roux*, the secret, some say, to really great Creole gravies.

In South Louisiana, fertile lands and mild climate encouraged production of a diversity of crops, and as in the North, the same plethora of wild game, fish, and crustaceans abounded in swamps, forests, rivers, and bayous. Southland fishermen could harvest oysters, speckled trout, shrimp, and crabs from the Gulf's salty depths and brackish coastal waters. Boiled or creamed; dressed in rice dishes or wine sauces; seafood was a lowland favorite in both city and country homes. Daily menus capitalized on foodstuffs "in season," and when possible, the excess was dried, pickled, smoked, or preserved.

Up and down the lower Mississippi, plantation families reveled in their self-sustained existence, enjoying delicious foods complimented by foreign liquors and Madeira wines. Using local cherries and grapes, these fun-loving colonists were even able to ferment a few spirits of their own. Coffee, tea, ice, and other luxuries were imported via the bustling port in New Orleans. Life was congenial and meals were the day's finest hours. A typical breakfast could offer fresh-picked strawberries; eggs poached in cream; and hot breads, brioches, beaten biscuits, or crusty French loaves—served with jellies, honey, and molasses. In Creole tradition, all meals were followed by cups of strong black chickory coffee or *café au lait* (coffee and milk). Dinner, the most elaborate meal, was served at night in New Orleans or in late afternoon on plantations.

The kitchen, together with smokehouse and milkhouse were ahum with constant activity and filled with pungent odors. The small complex of out-buildings was separated from, but easily accessible to, the manor house, in order to reduce the danger of fire. A huge fireplace covered the greater part of one kitchen wall and its insides were hung with swinging arms that held heavy iron cooking pots up to the fire. Roasting turkeys and game were dangled from ceiling hooks near the fire's heat and were periodically rotated by a small boy who also set out pans to catch their drippings. Gaping red ovens were built next to the fireplace while the remaining three walls held shelves and cupboards lined with crocks of spices, herbs, and preserved fruits. Sweets and cookies were wisely located on a high, swinging shelf to discourage mice and other nibblers. A table provided chopping space and a hideaway for tiny trespassers, whose eager faces peared from under the table or just outside the doorway if Mammy was "doing up a mess" of pralines or *la cuite* (heavy molasses) with pecans. A well-worn path connected this cooking area with the main house and was traditionally known as

"Whistler's Walk." Slaves carrying hot food from the kitchen were required to whistle as they hurried along; an activity that effectively prevented their sampling the dishes bound for the shining table of the master.

In the smokehouse beef was corned, pork became spareribs, and hams and sausage were hickory-smoked. Hickory chips in hampers lined the corners of this room and barrels of white lard and lye soap stood along the walls. Charcoal-insulated walls and a cooling stream were essential to the functioning of the milkhouse, the refrigerator of yesteryear. The milkhouse contained milk, large crocks of clabber, cream cheese, sour milk, and cream. Butter was tied in muslin bags and placed in crocks or stored in brine. Sometimes aspics for big meals were put to jell in the milkhouse.

Today, vestiges of the past remain an inherent part of Louisiana's charm. Daily menus are simpler, courses are fewer; yet red beans still simmer in the Monday pot, and rice and corn continue to support men and meals in their respective areas. The aroma of café noir lingers after every meal, and liquors and wines still overflow into the cooking pot as well as the wineglass. Tasty crawfish can be lured from flooded fields and narrow ditches and old-fashioned blacks still scan the country roadsides and New Orleans' grassy medians, picking pepper grass to season their pots. Louisiana's rich lands and waters continue to supply homes and restaurants with an impressive array of indigenous crops, fish, and game.

Exploring Louisiana's multifarious culinary heritage as it has evolved to the present is a pleasurable experience for native and visitor alike.

APPETIZERS—SOUPS AND GUMBOS

All recipes are for eight portions unless otherwise stated.

BAYOU CATFISH BITS

2 pounds catfish fillet*
Tabasco
Salt to taste
Pepper to taste

3 eggs, beaten
1½ cups corn meal
Cooking oil

Rub fish with Tabasco, salt, and pepper, and set aside for an hour or more. Cut fish into bite-size pieces; dip in eggs, then dredge in corn meal. Fry quickly in deep fat for 2 or 3 minutes, until golden brown. Drain on brown paper; serve on toothpicks at once. May be served alone or with a cocktail or remoulade sauce.

* Trout may be substituted for catfish.

CRABMEAT ROUNDS

1 pound crabmeat
2 green onions, minced
1 cup grated Cheddar cheese (sharp)

6 tablespoons homemade mayonnaise
50 toast rounds

Mix crabmeat, onions, cheese, and mayonnaise very gently. Correct seasoning. Put heaping teaspoon of mixture on each toast round; place in 450° oven for 8 minutes. Watch carefully.

CRAWFISH CARDINALE

3 green onions, bulb only, minced
6 tablespoons butter
2 tablespoons flour
1 cup light cream
¼ cup tomato ketchup
¾ teaspoon salt
¼ teaspoon white pepper

½ teaspoon Tabasco
2 teaspoons lemon juice
1 ounce brandy
1 pound boiled, peeled crawfish
  tails*
8 thin lemon slices
Paprika

In a skillet sauté onions in 4 tablespoons butter about 5 minutes. In a saucepan, melt 2 tablespoons butter. Blend in flour, add cream and ketchup, stirring constantly until sauce thickens. Add salt, pepper, Tabasco, and lemon juice. Flame brandy and slowly stir into sauce. Combine contents of both pans; add crawfish tails and stir. Divide the mixture into 8 ramekins and bake in 350° oven, until warm, approximately 12–15 minutes. Garnish with lemon slices and paprika.

* 1 pound cooked, peeled shrimp may be substituted for crawfish tails.

MARINATED SHRIMP

1½ cups salad oil
¾ cup white vinegar
1½ tablespoons salt
2½ tablespoons celery seeds

3 tablespoons capers
⅛ teaspoon Tabasco
2 cups sliced red onions (sliced
  in rings)

Prepare marinade by combining above ingredients and set aside.

3 quarts water
4 tablespoons salt

2 bags crab boil
2½ pounds peeled, uncooked
  shrimp

Combine water, salt, and crab boil in a large pot and bring to a fast boil. Add shrimp; let water return to boil then cook 2 minutes and remove from fire. Reserving liquid, remove shrimp, and place in a colander. Run cold water over shrimp to stop cooking. When liquid has cooled return shrimp and let soak for 1 hour. Drain shrimp and add to marinade and refrigerate at least 24 hours. Serve on toothpicks.

N.B. In place of crab boil you may use the following:

½ cup mustard seeds
½ cup coriander seeds
2 tablespoons dill seeds
2 tablespoons whole allspice

2 teaspoons crushed, dried red pepper
1 teaspoon ground cayenne
6 bay leaves

Tie the above ingredients in cheesecloth. Make sure the cheesecloth is large enough to allow for the expansion of seeds when they get wet.

LES ESCARGOTS

3 sticks butter
½ cup minced parsley
4 cloves garlic, pressed
2 teaspoons minced chives
Salt to taste

Pepper to taste
4 dozen snails
4 dozen snail shells
½ cup white wine

Combine butter, parsley, garlic, chives, salt, and pepper. Stuff about ¼ teaspoon of butter mixture into each shell, push snail far back into shell and put more butter mixture on top. Arrange shells in ramekins and pour 2 tablespoons wine in bottom of each dish. Bake in preheated 350° oven for 20 minutes.

MUSHROOMS MIREILLE

40 mushrooms, stems removed
1 stick butter
4 tablespoons finely chopped green onions
1½ cups crabmeat
3 tablespoons flour

1 cup milk
1 teaspoon salt
¼ teaspoon white pepper
2 tablespoons sherry (optional)
Paprika

Slightly sauté mushroom caps in 3 tablespoons butter. Transfer mushrooms to buttered baking dish. Sauté green onions in two tablespoons butter; remove from heat and add crabmeat. In another pan cook and stir flour in

3 tablespoons butter for 5 minutes, but do not brown. Heat milk and stir into cooked flour until smooth. Add salt, pepper, and sherry, and cook until sauce thickens. Mix in green onions and crabmeat. Correct seasoning. Stuff mushroom caps, sprinkle lightly with paprika, and bake in 350° oven for 15 minutes.

OYSTERS BIENVILLE

1 stick butter
1 cup finely chopped green onions
1 cup finely chopped yellow
  onions
6 ounces fresh raw mushrooms,
  finely chopped
2 tablespoons lemon juice
¼ cup flour
2 cups chicken consommé
1 cup dry white wine

1½ cups finely chopped raw
  shrimp
1 teaspoon salt
½ teaspoon white pepper
⅛ teaspoon cayenne
4 egg yolks
¼ cup whipping cream
8 pie pans
3 pounds ice cream salt
4 dozen oysters on the half shell

TOPPING—MIX:

¾ cup grated imported Parmesan
  cheese
¼ cup dry bread crumbs (plain)

¾ cup clarified butter
Paprika

In heavy 3-quart pot, melt butter. Add green and yellow onions. Sauté gently until wilted. Add mushrooms and lemon juice and continue to sauté, stirring frequently, for about ½ hour. Do not allow to brown. Remove pan from fire, sprinkle flour over contents. Stir until well blended. Return to fire, and over gentle flame slowly stir in consommé and white wine. Raise heat and continue cooking and stirring about 10 minutes until sauce has thickened. Add shrimp, salt, pepper and cayenne, and cook 5 more minutes. Remove from fire. Beat together egg yolks and whipping cream. Add a little warm sauce to yolk combination, then stir well back into mixture. Partially fill pie pans with ice cream salt. Pour off excess liquid from each oyster, place oyster and shell on ice cream salt (6 to a pan). Place in preheated 350° oven for 10 minutes. Remove pans from oven. Tip each shell to remove excess liquid and turn oven to 500°. Cover each oyster with sauce. Top each with mixture of cheese, bread crumbs, and butter. Sprinkle with paprika. Bake at 500° oven until brown—about 10 to 15 minutes.

OYSTERS AND ARTICHOKES

5 artichokes, boiled
1½ pints oysters (about 3 dozen)
2 cups water
2 sticks butter
½ cup flour
1¾ cup finely chopped onions
9 cloves garlic, minced
1 teaspoon thyme

2 teaspoons salt
½ teaspoon pepper
1 teaspoon lemon juice
¼ cup chopped parsley
Bread crumbs
8 thin slices lemon
Garnish: finely chopped parsley

Remove leaves from artichokes saving nice firm leaves to use as decoration and dippers. Scrape remaining leaves and reserve scrapings. Cut artichoke bottoms into eighths and place in ramekins. Drain oysters, reserving oyster liquor. Soak oysters in 2 cups water for at least 30 minutes; drain, reserving this liquid also. Make a dark brown roux with butter and flour; add onions and garlic, and sauté until tender, about 20 minutes. Add thyme, salt, pepper, artichoke scrapings and lemon juice. Slowly stir in oyster liquid (approximately 1½ cups). The gravy should be very thick. Simmer slowly for 45 minutes, stirring occasionally. Add oysters and parsley; cook 10 minutes. Remove from heat and spoon into ramekins. Best made ahead of time or night before. When ready to reheat, sprinkle with bread crumbs; top with lemon slices and thoroughly heat in 350° oven. Garnish with chopped parsley and surround ramekins with artichoke leaves. Use ¾-cup ramekins.

OYSTERS PIERRE

½ pound mushrooms, thinly
  sliced
1 stick butter
3 tablespoons flour
2 small garlic cloves, minced
3 tablespoons finely chopped
  green onions

3 tablespoons minced parsley
Dash of cayenne
1 teaspoon salt
⅓ cup good dry sherry
4 dozen small oysters, well
  drained
½ cup bread crumbs

Sauté mushrooms in 2 tablespoons butter and set aside. In a heavy skillet melt 4 tablespoons butter, add flour, and cook on low heat, stirring constantly, until light brown. Add garlic, green onions, parsley, and cook 5 minutes. Add cayenne, salt, and blend in sherry. Add oysters, mushrooms, and simmer 5 minutes. Transfer mixture to individual ramekins, top with bread crumbs, and dot with remaining butter. Heat in 350° oven until warm, about 15 minutes.

OYSTERS ROCKEFELLER

½ pound celery (about 4 stalks),
chopped
1 pound green onions (about 4
bunches), chopped
3 large cloves garlic, chopped
2½ sticks butter, melted
2 cups slightly cooked spinach,
chopped and well drained
4 tablespoons parsley, chopped
2 teaspoons salt
⅛ teaspoon cayenne

½ teaspoon ground anise seed (or
¼ cup Herbsaint)
1 tablespoon lemon juice
3 tablespoons Worcestershire
3 tablespoons ketchup
2 ounces anchovy fillets, mashed
to paste
Bread crumbs (optional)
8 pie pans
3 pounds ice cream salt
4 dozen oysters on the half shell

Sauté celery, green onions, and garlic in butter for five minutes. Remove from heat, add all other ingredients up to, but not including, bread crumbs, and mix well. Purée mixture one quarter at a time in blender. Mix all of purée together. Partially fill pie pans with ice cream salt. Pour off excess liquid from each oyster, place oyster and shell on salt (6 to a pan). Place in preheated 350° oven for 10 minutes. Remove pans from oven, turn oven to 500°. Tip each shell to remove excess liquid and cover each oyster with sauce. Bake at 500° for 15 minutes. Watch carefully. Slightly brown under broiler. Bread crumbs are used, if sauce needs thickening.

Alternate: This may be served from a chafing dish. Heat sauce. Drain oysters and place in a single layer in shallow pan and bake at 400° until just curled, about 5 or 6 minutes. Using a slotted spoon, transfer oysters to chafing dish and combine with sauce. This sauce freezes well.

SHRIMP MARINIÈRE

½ pound mushrooms, thinly
   sliced
1½ sticks butter
1 cup finely chopped green onions
5½ tablespoons flour
3 cups milk
1 teaspoon salt

½ teaspoon ground red pepper
   (not cayenne)
⅔ cup white wine
3 cups precooked shrimp
2 egg yolks, beaten
Paprika

Sauté mushrooms in 2 tablespoons butter and set aside. In a large, heavy skillet or Dutch oven, melt remaining butter, and sauté onions until tender. Blend in flour, and cook slowly for 5 minutes, stirring constantly. Remove from heat; gradually stir in milk until smooth. Add salt, pepper, and wine. Bring to a boil. Reduce heat; simmer and stir 10 minutes to thicken sauce. Add shrimp and mushrooms, stirring lightly for 1 minute. Remove from heat and quickly beat in egg yolks. Spoon into 8 ramekins, sprinkle with paprika, and heat under broiler. This can also be served from a chafing dish, over toast points.

SHRIMP REMOULADE

½ cup chopped onions
¾ cup oil
¼ cup tarragon vinegar
½ cup brown creole mustard
2 teaspoons paprika
¾ teaspoon cayenne pepper

2 teaspoons salt
2 medium cloves garlic, pressed
½ cup chopped green onion
2 pounds boiled, peeled shrimp
5 cups shredded lettuce

In a blender place onions, oil, vinegar, mustard, paprika, pepper, salt, and garlic. Blend 5 or 6 seconds, turn off, stir, blend another 5 or 6 seconds. Add green onions, and blend for 2 seconds. *Do not blend longer or you will have purée.* Chill sauce overnight. Arrange beds of lettuce on salad plates, top with shrimp, and cover with chilled sauce.

SHRIMP PÂTÉ

1 pound shrimp, boiled and peeled
¼ teaspoon salt
⅛ teaspoon pepper
⅛ teaspoon nutmeg*

⅛ teaspoon mace*
1 egg, beaten
⅔ cup white wine
6 tablespoons butter, softened

Grind shrimp in a blender, turning off and on to make sure all shrimp are finely ground. Add salt, pepper, nutmeg, mace, egg, and wine. Mix. Add butter, mixing well. Place in a lightly greased 2-cup mold or baking dish and bake in 350° oven for 50 minutes. Chill; unmold and serve with crackers.

* ½ teaspoon thyme and 2 tablespoons minced onions may be substituted for nutmeg and mace.

SALTED PECANS

½ stick butter
1 tablespoon salt

1 pound shelled pecans
½ teaspoon white pepper

Preheat oven to 350°. Melt butter in a shallow baking pan. Add pecans and stir well. Bake 20 minutes, stirring every five minutes. Remove from oven and sprinkle with salt and pepper. Let nuts cool in pan.

CHEESE STRAWS

15 ounces extra-sharp Cheddar
   cheese, grated
1½ sticks margarine†
2 cups plain flour
1¼ teaspoons baking powder

½ teaspoon salt
5 or 6 good dashes Tabasco
   (according to taste)
1 teaspoon cayenne pepper

Allow cheese and margarine to become room temperature before starting. Sift flour once; add baking powder and salt, resift and set aside. With hands, mix margarine and cheese well. Add Tabasco, cayenne and flour. Mix well.

Place this dough in a cookie press and press onto ungreased cookie sheets. Bake in preheated 300° oven for 10 minutes. Lower oven to 225° and cook until crisp (anywhere from 10 to 30 minutes). A specific time limit cannot be set, as ovens differ. If you think straws are cooking too fast, leave oven door open. Makes about 120 straws. These freeze well.

† Butter can be used, but straws will not keep as well, will be more brittle and slightly greasier.

HOT CHEESE PUFFS

4 ounces cream cheese
¾ teaspoon grated onions
¼ cup homemade mayonnaise
1 tablespoon chopped chives

⅛ teaspoon cayenne
⅛ cup Parmesan cheese
½ small loaf white bread

In a bowl, combine all ingredients except bread. Mix well. Cut bread into circles (1½″ rounds) and spread each with cheese mixture. Bake in 350° oven for 15 minutes; longer for a crispier puff. The bread may be cut and spread with cheese mixture, then frozen. Bake when ready to use.

ROQUEFORT CHEESE BALL

8 ounces cream cheese
8 ounces extra sharp Cheddar cheese
3 ounces Roquefort cheese

1 tablespoon Worcestershire sauce
1 small clove garlic, pressed
½ cup finely chopped pecans
½ cup minced parsley

Allow cheese to soften at room temperature. Break into pieces, add Worcestershire and garlic. Cream and thoroughly mix with an electric beater. Stir in ¼ cup pecans and chill until firm enough to shape into a ball. Cover ball with parsley and remaining pecans. Serve with crackers. Prepare a day before serving to allow flavors to blend. This freezes well.

ALMOND HAM ROLLS

8 ounces cream cheese, softened
¼ teaspoon dry mustard
¼ teaspoon paprika
⅛ teaspoon salt
⅛ teaspoon pepper
3 dashes Tabasco
1 teaspoon Worcestershire sauce
¼ teaspoon soy sauce

2 teaspoons chopped chives
2 tablespoons mayonnaise
1 tablespoon chopped almonds, or
   1 tablespoon finely chopped
   dill pickle
4 rectangular shaped slices of
   boiled ham, 6 by 3"

Toast almonds in 300° oven for 12–15 minutes or until brown. Mix cream cheese with all ingredients except ham and almonds. Add almonds to mixture. Dry ham on paper towels. Spread 3 tablespoons of mixture on each slice of ham, and roll lengthwise. Add a little mixture to ends of rolls if more filling is needed. Place in freezer 45 minutes or until rolls are hard enough to slice. Cut in ½" rounds. (These may be wrapped and frozen for 4 weeks.) Remove from freezer 1 hour before serving. Serve rounds on toothpicks or on crackers with a dash of mayonnaise.

Any of above ingredients may be altered to taste; however, amounts of mayonnaise and cream cheese remain the same.

CHICKEN LIVER PÂTÉ

1 pound livers, chicken or duck
¾ cup sliced mushrooms
   (save several for decoration)
2 sticks butter
¼ cup chopped green onions
¼ cup cognac
1 teaspoon salt

⅛ teaspoon freshly ground black
   pepper
⅛ teaspoon cayenne pepper
¼ teaspoon powdered allspice
⅛ teaspoon thyme
Chopped parsley for decoration

Wash, dry, and chop livers. Sauté mushrooms in butter for 5 minutes. Remove mushrooms with a slotted spoon and set aside. Sauté onions in same pan and cook 5 minutes. Add livers to pan, stir and cook until still barely pink inside, about 5 minutes. Put into blender; add mushrooms, cognac, and seasonings. If mixture is too thick, add more melted butter (1 or 2 tablespoons). Pack in crocks or a mold and chill. Serve in crock or unmold and decorate with parsley and mushrooms. Serve at room temperature. Freezes well.

MUSHROOM "FARCI"

40 mushrooms, 1–2" in diameter
  or 1 pound of larger mushrooms
½ cup grated Parmesan cheese
½ cup dry bread crumbs
¼ cup grated onions
2 small cloves garlic, minced
  (optional)

2 tablespoons chopped parsley
½ teaspoon salt
¼ teaspoon pepper
½ teaspoon oregano (optional)
1 stick butter, melted

Wash and dry mushrooms. Trim ends of stalks, then carefully remove stalks from caps. Chop stalks and mix with cheese, bread crumbs, onions, garlic, parsley, salt, pepper, and oregano. Fill mushroom caps with this mixture. (Do not overstuff.) Place caps in a shallow baking dish. Spoon butter over mushrooms, being sure to wet each cap. Bake in preheated 350° oven for 25 minutes.

CHILLED GREEN PEA SOUP

1 white medium onion, chopped
½ cup chopped celery
1 clove garlic, minced
3 tablespoons butter
1 quart beef stock
2 pounds freshly shelled green
  peas (weigh after shelling)
5 sprigs parsley, leaves only

½ teaspoon basil
¼ teaspoon thyme
1 bay leaf
1 quart heavy cream
Salt
White pepper
1½ ounces crème de menthe
Freshly chopped mint

In a large saucepan sauté onion, celery, and garlic in butter until golden brown. Add beef stock, fresh peas, parsley, basil, thyme, and bay leaf. Simmer until peas pop. Remove bay leaf and put soup through blender. Add cream, and season soup with salt and pepper. Stir in crème de menthe, and chill soup thoroughly. If soup is too thick at serving time, thin with milk. Sprinkle fresh mint on top.

CREAM OF ARTICHOKE SOUP

4 large or 6 medium artichokes
6 tablespoons butter
½ cup finely chopped onions
½ cup finely chopped celery
6 tablespoons flour
6 cups clear chicken broth
¼ cup lemon juice
1 bay leaf

1 teaspoon salt
¼ teaspoon pepper
¼ teaspoon thyme
2 egg yolks, beaten
2 cups light cream
Garnish: lemon slices chopped
　parsley

Boil artichokes for 1 hour. Scrape leaves and finely chop bottoms. In large saucepan sauté onion and celery in butter till soft but not brown. Add flour; cook 1 minute, stirring constantly. Add stock and lemon juice, stirring till blended. Add bay leaf, salt, pepper, thyme, artichoke scrapings and bottoms. Cover and simmer 20 minutes or until slightly thickened. At this stage soup may be puréed in blender if smooth, creamy consistency is desired. If serving hot, heat to boiling point, remove from heat, and add cream and egg yolks which have been beaten together. Correct seasoning and keep heated over hot water. If serving cold, add cream, egg yolks, correct seasoning, and chill. Serve garnished with thin lemon slices topped with parsley.

GAZPACHO

(Serves 4—Repeat for 8)

3 ripe tomatoes, peeled and
　quartered
⅓ cup chopped white onions
½ cup chopped green pepper
¼ cup chopped cucumber
2 teaspoons salt
1 clove garlic

¼ teaspoon white pepper
⅛ teaspoon Tabasco
1 teaspoon Worcestershire sauce
2 tablespoons olive oil
2 tablespoons lemon juice
¾ cup tomato juice

Place all ingredients in blender and purée. Press through a sieve to remove seeds. Chill thoroughly.

The following can be passed to be added to each serving:

2 cups toasted croutons

½ cup diced green pepper

2 diced tomatoes

1 diced cucumber

3 chopped hard-boiled eggs

OYSTER STEW

48 oysters

1½ cups oyster liquor and/or clam juice

1 stick butter

1 stick margarine

¼ cup chopped green onions

1½ cups finely chopped celery

½ teaspoon salt

½ teaspoon pepper

½ cup chopped curly parsley

5 tablespoons flour, sifted

3½ cups milk

Tabasco to taste

Drain oysters and save liquor. Melt butter and margarine in deep kettle. Sauté green onions and celery over medium flame until soft, about 20 minutes. Add salt and pepper. Stir occasionally. Add parsley, sauté 3 minutes. Add flour, stirring constantly until blended. Add oysters and liquor and remove from heat. Let stand 15 minutes. May be prepared in advance to this point. When reheating, do not let boil or oysters will shrink. Heat milk, being careful not to let it boil. Combine milk and oyster mixture, stirring constantly to blend. Add Tabasco and correct seasonings. Serve hot.

TURTLE SOUP

STOCK:

2 pounds turtle meat

1 gallon water

2 bay leaves

2 ribs celery, coarsely chopped

3 onions, quartered

2 carrots, coarsely chopped

4 sprigs parsley

6 cloves

½ teaspoon thyme

1 clove garlic

Boil turtle meat uncovered for approximately 2 hours in water seasoned with bay leaves, celery, onions, carrots, parsley, cloves, thyme, and garlic. Cook until meat is tender. Strain. If necessary add chicken or beef bouillon to make 3 quarts. Mince turtle meat and return to stock. This stock may be cooked the day before preparing soup.

SOUP:

¾ cup flour
½ cup butter or shortening
1 can tomatoes (16 ounces) seeded and puréed
6 tablespoons tomato sauce
½ cup finely chopped green onions
⅓ cup ground or finely chopped ham
½ cup sherry
3 tablespoons lemon juice

⅛ teaspoon cayenne pepper
½ teaspoon cinnamon
½ teaspoon nutmeg
Salt
Pepper
4 hard-boiled eggs (chopped)
8 lemon slices
¾ tablespoons chopped parsley
Extra sherry

In a soup kettle, make a medium brown roux of flour and melted butter or shortening. Add tomatoes, tomato sauce, and green onions. Simmer on low flame for 5 minutes, being careful not to let onions brown. Add ham, minced turtle meat, stock, and sherry. Simmer slowly, uncovered, for 2 hours. Add lemon juice, cayenne, cinnamon, nutmeg, salt, and pepper. Cook 5 minutes longer. Correct seasoning. To serve add 1 tablespoon sherry to each bowl and garnish with chopped eggs, lemon slices, and a pinch of parsley.

VICHYSSOISE

1½ cups diced leeks, white part only, or 1½ cups diced green onions, white part only
½ cup chopped onions
1 tablespoon butter
3–3½ cups peeled, diced baking potatoes

3 cups hot water
3 teaspoons salt
1 cup hot milk
½ teaspoon white pepper
1 cup light cream
1 cup heavy cream
8 teaspoons chopped chives

In a heavy 4-quart kettle cook leeks and chopped onions in butter until soft, but not brown. Add potatoes, hot water, and 2 teaspoons salt. Cook slowly, uncovered, for 30–40 minutes until potatoes are soft. Blend soup in blender until smooth and return to kettle. Add hot milk; carefully bring to a boil, stirring to keep from settling. Add 1 teaspoon salt, ½ teaspoon pepper; stir, remove from heat and strain through a sieve. Cool soup and stir to keep blended. Strain again and add light and heavy cream. Correct seasoning and chill. Serve garnished with chives.

CRAWFISH BISQUE

5 pounds live crawfish	Large pot boiling water
Cold water to cover	2 cups salt

In a container of cold water and 1 cup salt, purge live crawfish about 10 minutes. Rinse until water is clear. Drop crawfish into boiling salted water and boil for 10 minutes. Pick crawfish, reserving heads, shells, and fat. Clean 32 heads and set aside. Boil remaining heads and shells in 2 quarts of water for 15 minutes. Strain and reserve stock.

2 pounds picked crawfish tails	Pepper to taste
¼ pound butter	Cayenne to taste
2 cups finely chopped onions	2 cups bread crumbs
3 cloves finely chopped garlic	½ cup flour
1 cup finely chopped celery	2 16-ounce cans tomatoes
1 cup finely chopped green pepper	2 tablespoons lemon juice
½ cup bacon grease	3 bay leaves
½ cup finely chopped parsley	¼ teaspoon thyme
1½ cups bread, cubed	6 tablespoons tomato sauce
Salt to taste	Tabasco to taste

Grind crawfish tails. Sauté in butter about 5 minutes. If crawfish are very fat, cut down on the butter and substitute crawfish fat. In separate heavy pot, brown onions, garlic, celery, green pepper in ¼ cup bacon grease. Remove from fire. Add crawfish tails, parsley, bread cubes, and enough crawfish stock to soften mixture. Season with 1 teaspoon salt, ½ teaspoon black pepper, ¼ teaspoon cayenne and mix thoroughly. Stuff heads with mixture reserving the remainder. Roll heads in bread crumbs and place on a cookie sheet. In a 6-quart iron pot, make a dark brown roux using ¼ cup bacon grease and ½ cup flour. Add tomatoes, lemon juice, bay leaves, thyme, tomato sauce, remaining crawfish mixture and stock. Stir well, cover and cook on low fire about one hour or until mixture starts to thicken. Season with salt, pepper and Tabasco. Brown heads in 425° oven for 10 minutes, watching carefully. Add heads to bisque just before serving. If planning to freeze, freeze heads separately and add to bisque when heating to serve.

DUCK GUMBO

STOCK:

3 large ducks or 4 small ducks	2 carrots
1 gallon water	2 bay leaves
1 onion, quartered	3 teaspoons salt
2 ribs celery	1 teaspoon pepper

Skin ducks; boil in water with onion, celery, carrots, bay leaves, salt and pepper for approximately 1 hour or until duck meat is tender. Strain; skim all grease and reserve 3 quarts of stock. If needed, add chicken or beef bouillon to make 3 quarts stock. Remove meat from carcass and cut into bite-size pieces; return to stock. The stock may be made the day before making gumbo.

GUMBO:

¾ cup flour	1 pound okra cut in ¼″ pieces
¾ cup oil	2 tablespoons bacon grease
2 garlic cloves, minced	1 pound raw, peeled shrimp
1 cup finely chopped onions	1 pint oysters and liquor
½ cup finely chopped celery	¼ cup chopped parsley
1 cup finely chopped green peppers	2 cups cooked rice

In a large Dutch oven, make a dark brown roux with flour and oil. Add garlic, onions, celery, and green pepper; sauté uncovered on medium fire about ½ hour until onions are transparent. In separate skillet, sauté okra in bacon grease until all ropiness is gone, about 20 minutes; drain. In a soup pot warm stock and slowly stir in the roux and vegetable mixture. Add okra; simmer covered 1½ hours. Add shrimp, oysters and their liquor, and cook an additional 10 minutes. Stir in parsley and remove from fire. Correct seasoning and serve over hot, fluffy rice.

SEAFOOD GUMBO

STOCK:

5 quarts water
2 dozen boiled crabs
3 pounds raw shrimp
  (heads and shells on)

1 carrot
1 onion, quartered
½ cup coarsely chopped celery

Fill a 6-quart stock pot with 5 quarts of water. Pull off back shells of crabs, adding shells to stock pot. Discard inedible spongy fingers, break crabs in half, and set aside. Peel shrimp, adding heads and shells to pot. Set shrimp aside. To stock pot, add carrot, onion, celery, and cover, simmering for two hours. Strain stock, and return to pot.

GUMBO:

3 cups finely chopped onions
1½ cups finely chopped celery
1 cup finely chopped green
  peppers
3 cloves garlic, finely chopped
3 pounds okra, cut into ¼" pieces
1 cup and 1 tablespoon cooking
  oil
2 tablespoons flour
1 16-ounce can tomatoes, drained

½ cup diced ham or sausage
1 teaspoon thyme
1 teaspoon basil
3 bay leaves
¼ cup parsley, chopped
Salt
Pepper
Tabasco
Worcestershire sauce
2 cups cooked rice

Sauté onions, celery, green pepper, and garlic in ¼ cup oil until soft. Fry okra separately in ¾ cup of oil over medium flame, about 45 minutes or until soft and ropy texture is gone. Stir often. More oil can be added if okra sticks. In separate frying pan, make brown roux with 1 tablespoon oil and 2 tablespoons flour. Add tomato pulp and cook into a paste. Add ham, thyme, basil, and bay leaves. Cook for 5 minutes. Add sautéed seasoning and okra to stock and while stirring, slowly add the roux mixture. Simmer for 1 hour. Add peeled shrimp, crab halves, parsley, and cook an additional ½ hour. Season with salt, pepper, Tabasco, and Worcestershire sauce to taste. Freezes beautifully. Serve in gumbo bowls over rice.

TURKEY GUMBO

1 turkey carcass
4 tablespoons flour
4 tablespoons bacon grease
1 cup chopped green onions
1 cup chopped celery
4 tablespoons chopped parsley
2–3 bay leaves
½ teaspoon thyme

1 cup chopped sausage
   (hot, smoked)
3 cups turkey meat from carcass
Salt to taste
Pepper to taste
1 pint oysters and liquid
1 tablespoon gumbo filé
2 cups cooked rice

In a soup kettle, cover turkey carcass with at least 8 cups of water and boil about 1 hour, or until meat is easily removed from the bone. Remove carcass and pick meat off of bone. Strain and reserve 6 cups of turkey broth. To make roux, brown flour in bacon grease until mixture is a rich dark brown. Add onions, celery, and parsley; sauté 5 minutes. Slowly add broth to roux; add bay leaves, thyme, sausage, and turkey meat. Salt and pepper to taste and cook over low heat 1½–2 hours, adding oysters for last 5 minutes of cooking. Add filé just before serving, being careful not to let mixture boil once it has been added. Remove bay leaves and serve over hot rice. If planning to freeze, do not add oysters and filé until reheating to serve.

EGGS AND CHEESE

All recipes are for eight portions unless otherwise stated.

CONGÉ EGGS

8 English muffins, halved
16 thin slices grilled ham
16 slices grilled tomato
1 recipe Marchand de Vin sauce
  (see index)
16 soft poached eggs

1 recipe Hollandaise sauce
  (see index)
Salt to taste
Pepper to taste
Paprika to taste

Butter English muffins and toast lightly. Lay a slice of ham followed by a slice of tomato on each half of English muffin. Cover this with the Marchand de Vin sauce and then add the poached egg. Eggs may be lightly sprinkled with salt and pepper before covering them with Hollandaise sauce. Garnish with paprika. Serve immediately.

EGGS SARDOU

16 boiled artichokes
½ cup chopped green onions
1 stick butter
4 cups cooked spinach, drained
1 pint sour cream
¼ cup Parmesan cheese
2 tablespoons lemon juice

Salt to taste
Pepper to taste
Worcestershire sauce to taste
16 eggs
2 cups Hollandaise sauce
  (see index)

Scrape the leaves of 8 artichokes and reserve scrapings. Remove all 16 artichoke bottoms and place in a greased, ovenproof dish. Sauté onions in butter. Add spinach, stir in sour cream, Parmesan cheese, lemon juice, salt, pepper, Worcestershire, and artichoke scrapings. Mix well. Place some of the spinach mixture on each artichoke bottom and heat thoroughly in 350° oven. Meanwhile poach eggs and place 1 egg on each artichoke bottom. Serve immediately, topping each with Hollandaise sauce, and garnish with paprika if desired.

OEUFS AUX CHAMPIGNONS

12 hard-boiled eggs
1 pint fresh mushrooms, minced
1 stick butter
Salt
White and red pepper
Worcestershire sauce and Tabasco
½ pound bacon, crisp-fried and
*   crumbled*

½ pound sharp cheese, grated
¼ cup flour
2 cups milk
2 tablespoons sherry
2 tablespoons minced parsley
Paprika

Slice eggs lengthwise; remove yolks to mixing bowl and mash until smooth. Sauté mushrooms in ½ stick of butter. Add ½ of sautéed mushrooms and butter to egg yolks. Season mixture highly with salt, peppers, Worcestershire, and Tabasco. Stuff egg whites with mixture and press two halves together. Arrange in a lightly greased round casserole. Top with remaining mushrooms, half of bacon and half of cheese. Make cream sauce with flour, milk, and ½ stick butter. Season sauce highly with salt, pepper, Worcestershire, and Tabasco. Add sherry. Pour over eggs. Top with remaining bacon and cheese. May be refrigerated at this point. Bring casserole to room temperature. Bake in 350° oven for 25–30 minutes, until bubbly. Garnish with parsley and paprika.

OEUFS AU VIN

1 cup diced, sliced ham
¾ cup sliced mushrooms
5½ tablespoons butter
1 cup chopped white onions
1 garlic clove on toothpick
2 tablespoons flour
10½ ounces beef stock
10½ ounces red wine

1/16 teaspoon thyme
1 sprig parsley
¼ teaspoon white pepper
8 eggs
8 slices French bread (½" thick)
*   fried in butter*
Garnish: water cress or parsley

In heavy frying pan, sauté ham and mushrooms in 1½ tablespoons butter for 3 minutes. Remove ham and mushrooms with slotted spoon and reserve. Add 3 tablespoons butter and sauté onions for several minutes, add garlic, remove from heat and stir in flour. Return to heat and add stock, wine, thyme, parsley, and pepper. Simmer 20 minutes. It will still be thin. Return ham and mushrooms to sauce and boil several minutes until it is slightly thick. Remove garlic and parsley and check seasoning. Poach eggs in salted water. Place on fried French bread and keep warm in 150° oven until all eggs are poached. Spoon sauce over eggs and bread, garnish with sprigs of water cress or parsley, and serve at once.

BASIC OMELETTE

3 eggs
1 tablespoon water
½ teaspoon salt

Dash of pepper
2–3 drops Tabasco
1 tablespoon clarified butter

Slightly beat eggs; mix in water; add salt, pepper, and Tabasco. Heat butter in an omelette pan. When butter sizzles, add eggs. When eggs begin to set, lower heat. When omelette is set, loosen edges and fold two sides toward the center. Slide onto warm plate. This recipe serves 1 person amply.

CRABMEAT OMELETTE

1½ tablespoons chopped green
   onions
1½ teaspoons chopped parsley
1½ teaspoons butter
½ cup lump crabmeat

Salt to taste
Pepper to taste
Tabasco to taste
1 teaspoon lemon juice
Basic omelette (see index)

Sauté green onions and 1 teaspoon parsley in butter until soft, being careful not to let butter brown. Add crabmeat, tossing lightly so as not to break up lumps. Season to taste and add lemon juice. Prepare basic omelette. When eggs begin to set, add crabmeat mixture and turn down heat. When omelette is set, fold two sides toward center, over filling. Garnish with remaining parsley. Serves 1.

CREOLE OMELETTE

⅓ cup Creole sauce (see index)   Basic omelette (see index)

Heat Creole sauce. Prepare basic omelette; slide onto warm plate and pour on Creole sauce. Serves 1.

TOMATO NESTS

8 large tomatoes
1 stick butter
8 tablespoons finely chopped
   green onions
6 tablespoons finely chopped
   parsley
3 tablespoons finely chopped
   celery
1½ cups sliced mushrooms
2 cups fresh bread crumbs
2 tablespoons water

Salt to taste
Pepper to taste
Cayenne pepper to taste
Worcestershire sauce to taste
Tabasco to taste
Softened butter
8 raw eggs
8 Holland Rusks
8 slices pimento
Parsley to garnish
Paprika to garnish

Wash tomatoes; top and scoop them out; turn them upside down to drain. In a skillet, melt butter and sauté green onions, parsley, celery, and mushrooms until onions are soft. Add bread crumbs which have been moistened with water. Season well with salt, pepper, cayenne, Worcestershire and Tabasco. Cook stuffing to desired consistency. Salt tomato shells inside and rub the outside with softened butter. Fill each tomato shell with stuffing, allowing room for a poached egg to be placed on top. Arrange in a lightly greased dish and place in 350° oven for about 25 minutes. Poach eggs and place one in each cooked tomato. Serve on Holland Rusk, topping each egg with a slice of pimento. Sprinkle with paprika and parsley.

OYSTER OMELETTE

2 ½ tablespoons butter
½ cup mushrooms, sliced
1 ½ tablespoons flour
¼ cup finely chopped green onions
¼ cup finely chopped parsley
¼ cup sherry
½ cup oyster liquor

2–2 ½ dozen oysters, well drained
Salt to taste
Pepper to taste
Tabasco to taste
Worcestershire sauce to taste
Basic omelette (see index)

In 1 tablespoon butter, sauté mushrooms until liquid has evaporated; set aside. Add remaining butter and flour to pan, and when lightly browned, add green onions and parsley; cook until onions are soft. Add sherry and oyster liquor; stir and cook until mixture has a creamy consistency. Add well-drained oysters and mushrooms, and cook until oysters begin to curl, approximately 2–3 minutes. Add salt, pepper, Tabasco, and Worcestershire to taste. Keep sauce warm in double boiler while preparing omelettes. Prepare omelettes, slide onto warm plates, and top with oyster sauce. This is enough sauce for 4 basic omelettes.

CHEESE SOUFFLÉ

4 tablespoons butter
3 tablespoons flour
1 ½ cups half-and-half cream
1 teaspoon salt
¼ teaspoon cayenne
¼ teaspoon dry mustard

¼ teaspoon ground nutmeg
2 cups grated sharp Cheddar
    cheese*
6 egg yolks
8 egg whites
¼ teaspoon cream of tartar

Over low heat melt butter and add flour, stirring with a wooden spoon until blended. Slowly add cream, stirring constantly. Heat until thick, but do not let mixture boil. Add salt, cayenne, mustard, nutmeg, 1½ cups of cheese, and blend. Beat egg yolks two at a time; add to mixture, blending after each addition; place in a large bowl. Add cream of tartar to egg whites before beating, and beat until stiff. Butter a 2-quart soufflé dish and sprinkle lightly with grated cheese. Fold egg whites into cheese mixture and turn into soufflé

* Other cheeses may be used.

dish. Sprinkle top with remaining grated cheese. Set dish in a pan of hot water (not boiling) and place in a cold oven. Set oven at 325° and bake for 40 to 50 minutes. Top should be a delicate brown crust.

LORRAINE CUSTARD

8 strips bacon	4 eggs
2 cups light cream, room temperature	Salt to taste
	Pepper to taste
4 ounces Gruyère cheese, grated	Tabasco to taste
4 ounces Parmesan cheese, grated	⅛ teaspoon nutmeg

Fry bacon until crisp, drain on absorbent paper, and crumble into small pieces. Place in bottom of 8 ramekins (½-cup size). To light cream, add the grated cheese and stir well. Beat eggs and add slowly to cream and cheese mixture. Season with salt, pepper, Tabasco, and nutmeg. Pour into ramekins and set these dishes in a pan of hot but not boiling water and bake in 450° oven until custard is set and lightly colored, approximately 20 minutes. This is an excellent first course.

ONION PIE

CRUST:

A regular 9" pie crust, baked, or
Mix 1 cup Saltine cracker crumbs with ¼ cup butter and press into 9" pie pan.

FILLING:

3 cups diced onion	1 teaspoon salt
¼ cup butter	¼ teaspoon cayenne
½ pound Swiss cheese, finely grated	3 eggs, beaten well
	1 cup scalded milk
1 tablespoon flour	

Sauté onions in butter, slowly, stirring constantly until golden. Remove from fire; drain and put into pie shell. Combine cheese, flour, salt, and cayenne; stir in eggs and milk. Pour over onions and bake in 350° oven for 40 minutes.

QUICHE LORRAINE

1 9" pastry shell, baked until
  lightly browned
¼ cup ham, cooked and chopped
1 medium onion, sliced
¾ cup chopped Swiss cheese
½ cup sliced mushrooms
2 tablespoons butter

1 tablespoon flour
1 cup milk, warmed
2 eggs, well beaten
Salt to taste
Red pepper to taste
Nutmeg to taste

Place ham in bottom of pastry shell. Cook onions in salted water until limp. Drain and place on ham, and sprinkle cheese over ham and onions. Sauté mushrooms in 1 tablespoon of butter and spread over mixture. Set aside and prepare custard. Melt 1 tablespoon butter. Remove from stove and add flour very slowly, stirring constantly until smooth. Return to fire. Cook 3 minutes on low heat. Add warm milk to butter slowly, approximately 1 tablespoon at a time, cooking slowly and stirring constantly until slightly thickened. Let cool, then add 2 eggs. Season with salt, red pepper, and nutmeg, and pour over other ingredients. Bake at 350° until firm. Approximately 30 minutes.

WELSH RAREBIT

9 ounces beer
1½ pounds sharp Cheddar cheese,
  grated

1½ teaspoons salt
½ teaspoon cayenne pepper
2 eggs, beaten

Warm beer in top of double boiler; then, using a wire whisk, slowly stir cheese into beer and mix constantly over low heat until no lumps appear and beer and cheese are thoroughly blended. Add salt, pepper, and beaten eggs. (Add some cheese mixture to the eggs, to warm them, before adding the eggs to the cheese.) Cook until thick. If mixture should curdle, put it in blender and blend on high speed. This keeps in refrigerator for weeks.

VEGETABLES AND RICE

All recipes are for eight portions unless otherwise stated.

CABBAGE FRANÇAIS

1 green cabbage (1½–2 pounds)
   chopped*
Water to cover
3 tablespoons butter
¼ cup flour
1 cup whipping cream
½ cup milk

½ teaspoon salt
⅛ teaspoon white pepper
⅛ teaspoon red pepper
⅛ teaspoon nutmeg
2 tablespoons butter (for topping)
Bread crumbs
Grated Parmesan cheese

Cook cabbage in boiling water until tender, approximately 7 minutes. Drain well. Melt butter; blend in flour; add cream and milk, slowly stirring constantly until sauce thickens. Stir in salt, white and red pepper, and nutmeg. Remove from heat and stir in vegetable. Pour into 1½-quart buttered baking dish, dot with butter, and sprinkle with cheese. Bake in 375° oven for 20–25 minutes.

* Two small cauliflower heads, cut into small florets, may be substituted.

BROCCOLI AU GRATIN

2 cups milk
4 tablespoons flour
16 ounces cream cheese—room
   temperature
1 ounce Roquefort cheese—room
   temperature

1 teaspoon salt
½ teaspoon pepper
2½ pounds fresh broccoli
½ cup bread crumbs
½ stick butter

Heat milk. Blend in flour, cream cheese, Roquefort, salt, pepper, and stir over low heat until smooth. Cook broccoli until barely tender. Drain and place in 3-quart casserole and pour cheese sauce over broccoli. This much may be prepared the day before. Bake in 350° oven for 50 minutes. Top with bread crumbs, dot with butter, and return to oven for 10 minutes.

ASPARAGUS WITH SOUR CREAM

> 3 pounds fresh asparagus
> 1½ cups chicken broth

> 5 strips bacon, crisply fried and crumbled
> 2 hard-boiled egg yolks, chopped

Prepare asparagus by cutting off ends and tying stalks together. Place in pot, add chicken broth; cover, and cook until tender. Drain and transfer to a warm buttered baking dish. Prepare sauce.

SAUCE:

> 1 cup sour cream
> 2 eggs, lightly beaten
> 1 tablespoon lemon juice

> 1 tablespoon sweet vermouth
> Salt to taste
> Pepper to taste

In a saucepan over low heat, slowly blend sour cream, eggs, and lemon juice, stirring constantly with a wire whisk. When slightly warm, stir in vermouth, salt and pepper. Sauce takes approximately 6 minutes to make. Pour sauce over warm asparagus and serve topped with crumbled bacon and chopped egg yolks.

CELERY PONTALBA

> 6 cups celery, cut in 1" pieces
> Salted water
> 4½ tablespoons butter
> 4½ tablespoons flour
> 1½ cups milk
> 1½ tablespoons finely chopped celery plus leaves

> 1½ tablespoons chopped green pepper
> ⅛ teaspoon onion salt
> ⅛ teaspoon pepper
> 1 teaspoon salt

Cook pieces of celery in salted water until tender. Drain and set aside. Melt butter in a saucepan, add flour, and blend well. Add milk slowly, stirring constantly, until sauce thickens. Add finely chopped celery, green pepper, onion salt, pepper, and salt; simmer 2 minutes. Add drained celery; simmer 5 minutes.

CREAMED SPINACH

½ cup chopped green onions
1 stick butter
4 cups cooked, drained, and
    salted spinach
1 pint sour cream
¼ cup Parmesan cheese

2 tablespoons lemon juice
¼ teaspoon garlic salt
3 artichokes, boiled, leaves
    scraped and bottoms cut into
    small pieces
½ cup buttered bread crumbs

Sauté green onions in butter and add to drained spinach. Stir in sour cream, cheese, lemon juice, garlic salt, and then add artichoke scrapings and bottoms. Lightly grease a 2-quart baking dish and pour in mixture. Sprinkle with buttered bread crumbs and bake in 350° oven until bubbly, approximately 30 minutes.

GRATED CORN PUDDING

2¼ cups milk
1 stick butter, melted
8 ears corn, grated, or 3–4 cups
    corn
4 eggs, well beaten

2 tablespoons sugar
2 teaspoons salt
½ teaspoon white pepper
2 drops Tabasco

Scald milk, remove from heat, and add rest of ingredients. Mix well. Recipe may be prepared several hours ahead of time to this point. Stir well and pour into a 2-quart greased baking dish. Place baking dish in a pan half filled with warm water, and bake at 325° for approximately 1 hour and 15 minutes. Pudding is done when knife comes out clean from center of dish.

MAQUE CHOUX

¾ cup chopped onions
¾ cup bacon grease
10 ears fresh corn, kernels cut
 from cob

4 Creole or fresh tomatoes,
 peeled and chopped
⅓ cup minced green pepper
1 teaspoon salt
1 teaspoon black pepper

Sauté onions in bacon grease until transparent, about 5 minutes. Add corn and cook 10 minutes, stirring constantly. Add tomatoes and green pepper and cook 5 minutes, or until very soft. Add salt and pepper. May be served like this or as a stuffing in a cooked green pepper or tomato.

PLANTAINS

8–10 plantains or green-tipped
 bananas
2 sticks butter

¾ cup light brown sugar
½ cup dark rum

Peel and quarter plantains, placing split side up in a shallow baking dish. Dot plantains with slices of butter; sprinkle with sugar and rum. Bake covered in a 350° oven for 30 minutes. Remove cover and cook at 400° for an additional 15 minutes. Serve. If using bananas, bake in an uncovered shallow dish at 350° for a total of 20 minutes.

STUFFED MIRLITONS

5 medium-size mirlitons*
⅓ cup minced onions
⅔ cup chopped green onions
3 cloves garlic, minced
¼ cup chopped parsley
¾ cup melted ham fat or bacon
 grease
1 cup ham or raw shrimp, chopped
 or ½ cup each

¾ cup fresh bread crumbs
½ teaspoon salt (1 teaspoon if
 shrimp are used)
½ teaspoon pepper
1 pinch minced hot pepper or
 2 dashes Tabasco
1 egg, beaten

Cover mirlitons with water and boil until tender, about 1 hour. Cool and cut in half lengthwise. Scoop out tender pulp and reserve. Discard seeds and set shells aside for stuffing. Sauté onions, green onions, garlic, and parsley in ½ cup fat for 5 minutes, or until onions are transparent. Add ham or shrimp, and cook, stirring for 5 minutes. Add mirliton pulp, ½ cup bread crumbs, salt, pepper, hot pepper, and cook, stirring 10 minutes. Add ¼ cup fat if mixture is dry. Turn off fire and stir thoroughly. Add egg, return to heat, and cook 1 minute. Fill 8 shells and sprinkle with remaining bread crumbs. Bake in 375° oven for 10 to 15 minutes, or until bread crumbs have browned. Mirlitons may be prepared ahead of time. They freeze well.

* Mirlitons are vegetable pears. If unavailable, summer squash can be substituted.

SWEET POTATOES IN ORANGES

8 medium sweet potatoes
1 stick butter
¾ cup light brown sugar
4 beaten eggs
1 cup light cream
⅛ teaspoon ground allspice

¼ teaspoon ground cinnamon
1 teaspoon salt
½ cup chopped pecans
½ cup Sherry
8 orange cups†

Bake potatoes at 350° for 60 minutes, until soft. Peel potatoes and mash well, removing all lumps. While hot add butter, sugar, eggs, cream, allspice, cinnamon, and salt. Stir in pecans and sherry, reserving a few pecans for decoration. Place in oranges, decorate with pecans, and bake in a 350° oven for 20 minutes to brown top.

† To make orange cups, cut 4 large oranges in half, scoop out all pulp without damaging rind. Flute the edges of each cup.

TANGY GREEN BEANS

80 long pole or green beans (1½–2 pounds)
8 slices bacon, partially cooked
8 toothpicks

In well-seasoned water partially cook beans. Secure 10 beans in a bundle wrapped with bacon and fixed with a toothpick. Place on a foil-covered cookie sheet and bake in 400° oven until bacon is done on all sides, approximately 10–15 minutes. Pour sauce over beans and serve hot.

SAUCE:

3 tablespoons bacon grease

2 tablespoons cider vinegar

2 tablespoons tarragon vinegar

1 teaspoon salt

½ teaspoon paprika

1 tablespoon chopped parsley

1 teaspoon grated onions

Boil above ingredients over medium flame for 5 minutes. Put 1 tablespoon of sauce over each bundle of beans. Remove toothpicks before serving.

TOMATOES WITH ARTICHOKE

4 large, firm tomatoes

4 artichokes, boiled in salted
   water

1 stick butter

¼ teaspoon thyme

1 clove garlic, crushed

1 bay leaf

2 teaspoons lemon juice

1 teaspoon salt

½ teaspoon pepper

Parmesan cheese

1 cup vermouth

Wash and dry tomatoes. Cut out stems, leaving as small a hole as possible, and cut tomatoes in half crosswise. Scoop out half of the pulp and reserve. Turn shells upside down to drain excess juices. Salt and pepper inside of shells and place a thin slice of butter in each; arrange in a buttered casserole dish. Scrape artichoke leaves and dice bottoms. In a skillet melt 4 tablespoons butter, add artichoke scrapings and bottoms, tomato pulp, thyme, garlic and bay leaf; sauté about 10 minutes over medium flame. Mash. Add lemon juice, salt, and pepper. Remove bay leaf. Place about 2 tablespoons of artichoke mixture in each tomato. Top generously with Parmesan cheese. Recipe may be done ahead, to this point. Pour vermouth in bottom of pan and bake in 400° oven for 25 minutes. Arrange on a serving platter and top each with a little of the pan liquid.

TOMATOES STUFFED WITH MUSHROOMS

8 medium-size tomatoes, firm but
　ripe
1 stick butter
1¼ pounds mushrooms, sliced
1 cup sour cream
4 teaspoons flour
1½ ounces Roquefort cheese—
　room temperature

1 teaspoon chopped parsley
2 tablespoons dry sherry
Salt to taste
Pepper to taste
Worcestershire—a dash
8 teaspoons ground almonds
　(optional)
Paprika

Wash tomatoes. Slice off tops, spoon out soft insides, and turn shells upside down to drain. Melt butter and sauté mushrooms until moisture has evaporated. Blend sour cream and flour with mushrooms, and cook over low heat until thick and bubbly. Add Roquefort and stir until smooth. Add parsley, sherry, salt, pepper, Worcestershire, and let cool. Stuff shells, sprinkle with almonds and paprika, and bake in 375° oven until bubbly, about 15 to 20 minutes. Serve immediately.

STEWED OKRA AND TOMATOES

3 pounds fresh okra, thinly
　sliced
⅓ cup bacon drippings
2 cups finely chopped onions
1 clove garlic, pressed
½ cup finely chopped celery
1 cup finely chopped green pepper
1 bay leaf

2 pounds ripe Creole tomatoes,
　peeled and cut into small
　pieces
1 teaspoon salt
⅛ teaspoon thyme
3 to 4 dashes Tabasco
Pepper to taste
½ pound bacon, crisply fried and
　crumbled

Fry okra in bacon drippings, stirring often, until there is no sign of ropiness, about 30 minutes. Add onions, garlic, celery, green pepper, bay leaf, and cook until onions are transparent, about 15 minutes. Add tomatoes, and cook 10 minutes. Add salt, thyme, Tabasco, and pepper. Simmer, covered, for 30 minutes. Remove bay leaf and serve garnished with bacon.

YELLOW SQUASH WITH PEAS

6 to 8 small yellow squash
10 ounces shelled green peas
2 tablespoons butter
1 teaspoon salt
½ teaspoon white pepper

2 tablespoons light cream
1 teaspoon sugar
2 tablespoons fresh bread crumbs
2 tablespoons Parmesan cheese

Parboil squash until tender, about 4–5 minutes. Drain, cut in half lengthwise, and form a cavity by scooping out seeds. Cook peas, and place in blender with butter, salt, pepper, cream, and sugar. Blend. Should be soft but still hold shape. Add more cream if mixture is too stiff. Fill cavities with purée and place squash in a greased shallow baking dish. Top each with bread crumbs and cheese and bake in 350° oven for 15–18 minutes. This may be prepared the day before using.

ZUCCHINI CASSEROLE

2 onions, thinly sliced
6 tablespoons butter
2 pounds zucchini, thinly sliced
2 medium-size tomatoes thinly sliced

Salt to taste
Pepper to taste
¼ cup grated Parmesan cheese

Sauté onions in butter until yellow. Add zucchini; cook and stir 5 minutes. Add tomatoes, salt, and pepper. Cover and cook 5 minutes. Either reduce heat and cook until tender, approximately 25 minutes, or transfer to a casserole, sprinkle with grated cheese, and bake in 375° oven until browned. Approximately 45 minutes to 1 hour. This may be prepared the day before serving.

BAKED GRITS

1½ cups grits*
6 cups water
2½ teaspoons salt
1 stick butter

¼ teaspoon cayenne
3 eggs, beaten
1 pound sharp cheese, grated
1 tablespoon chopped parsley

* Grits is the coarse meal made from hulled and ground corn.

Add grits to boiling salted water, and cook until done. Add butter, cayenne, eggs, and 14 ounces of cheese, mixing well. Pour into a buttered 2½-quart baking dish; top with remaining cheese, and bake 1 hour and 15 minutes in a 350° oven. Garnish with parsley.

GARLIC GRITS

2 cups grits
2 quarts water
3 teaspoons salt
6 ounces American cheese, grated
3 cloves garlic, pressed

1 stick butter
3 eggs, slightly beaten
2 cups milk
Grated Parmesan cheese

Cook grits in boiling salted water until tender but still pourable. Remove from heat; add cheese, garlic, and butter, stirring until melted. When cool, add eggs and milk. Pour into two 2-quart casseroles that have been well greased. Bake in 325° oven for 50–60 minutes. Remove from oven; sprinkle with Parmesan cheese and bake for about 10 more minutes. Serve immediately. This may be prepared ahead. Keep refrigerated and bake before serving.

COUNTRY DIRTY RICE

½ cup oil
3 tablespoons flour
1 cup finely chopped onions
1½ pounds finely chopped chicken
    livers
½ cup chopped celery
½ cup finely chopped parsley
1 cup chopped green onions

½ cup chopped green pepper
1 teaspoon minced garlic
Salt to taste
Pepper to taste
⅛ teaspoon cayenne pepper
4½ cups stock
2 cups long-grain rice

In a Dutch oven make a brown roux with oil and flour. Add white onions, and stir until brown. Add chicken livers, celery, parsley, green onions, green pepper, garlic; and stir. Add salt, pepper, and cayenne. Cook for 5 minutes over medium heat; then add ½ cup stock and cook an additional 15 minutes. Skim excess oil from top of mixture and remove from heat. In a separate pan cook 2 cups rice in 4 cups stock until fluffy. Fold rice into vegetable mixture and correct seasoning. To serve warm in 350° oven for 20 minutes.

OAK ALLEY SPOON BREAD

4 cups milk
1 cup white corn meal
1½ teaspoons salt
2 teaspoons baking powder

2 teaspoons sugar
2 tablespoons butter
6 eggs, separated

Heat milk to boiling point; slowly add corn meal, and cook until very soft. Take off fire and add salt, baking powder, sugar, and butter. Beat until cool. Add egg yolks, one at a time, and beat well. Fold in stiffly beaten egg whites. Bake in two greased 2-quart baking dishes for ½ hour in 400° oven.

GREEN RICE

2 cups rice
6 cups water
Salt to taste
2 bay leaves
½ cup chopped onions

¼ cup minced green onions
1 stick butter
½ cup chopped parsley
1 cup chopped celery

Cook rice in salted water with bay leaves. Drain and remove bay leaves. Place in colander and steam until fluffy. Sauté onions and green onions in butter until well done. Add parsley and celery, cooking slightly. Celery should remain crisp. Add cooked rice; mix well. Heat to serve, or put in a baking dish and heat in 350° oven for 20 minutes.

LOUISIANA HERB RICE

4 tablespoons butter
3 tablespoons minced onions
1 teaspoon minced garlic
2 cups raw rice
2 bay leaves
1 teaspoon thyme

½ teaspoon basil
1 teaspoon marjoram
4 cups chicken stock
Salt to taste
Pepper to taste

Melt butter in a saucepan and sauté onions and garlic without browning. Add rice, bay leaves, thyme, basil, and marjoram. Cook until translucent.

Bring stock to a boil and add to rice. Salt and pepper to taste; cover and simmer 30 minutes or until tender. Remove bay leaves before serving.

RED RICE

1 stick butter	2 cups uncooked rice
1 cup finely chopped onions	2 teaspoons salt
½ cup finely chopped celery	¼ teaspoon cayenne pepper
¾ cup tomato paste	4 cups chicken stock
⅓ cup water	2 ounces of pimentos

In a skillet melt ½ stick butter and sauté onion and celery until limp. Add tomato paste and water. Cover and simmer 20 minutes. In a Dutch oven melt ½ stick butter and sauté rice until translucent. Add salt, pepper, and stock to rice. Cover and simmer 15 minutes. Add sauce and pimentos; cook until rice is tender, approximately 10 minutes.

RIZ AUX ÉPINARDS

1 stick butter	5 teaspoons chopped celery
¼ cup chopped chives	4 teaspoons sherry (optional)
5 teaspoons chopped parsley	5 cups cooked rice
1 cup cooked, chopped spinach	1 teaspoon salt

In a large skillet melt butter, and sauté chives, parsley, spinach, and celery over medium flame until limp. Reduce heat and add sherry, stirring constantly. Slowly add rice; remove from flame when warmed and add salt.

WILD RICE AND OYSTERS

5 cups beef stock	1 cup dry white wine
10 tablespoons butter	¼ cup minced parsley
2 cups wild rice	½ teaspoon each: thyme, oregano,
½ cup minced green pepper	sweet basil, sweet marjoram
1 garlic clove, pressed	2 teaspoons salt
2 tablespoons minced celery	¼ teaspoon white pepper
2 cups sliced mushrooms	2 cups oysters, well drained

In large saucepan bring beef stock, 2 tablespoons butter, and the rice to a boil. Cook over low heat for 25–35 minutes. Drain. Put in colander and steam until tender. In 4 tablespoons of butter sauté green pepper, garlic, and celery until limp. Add mushrooms and wine; simmer 15 minutes. Add parsley, thyme, oregano, basil, marjoram, salt, and pepper. Mix rice with seasoning by the spoonful. Transfer to a 3-quart baking dish. Dip oysters in 4 tablespoons melted butter and place on top of rice. Bake uncovered 30 minutes in 350° oven.

PASTA MILANAISE

1½ cups sliced fresh mushrooms
1 stick butter
2 tablespoons flour
1 pint half-and-half cream
1 cup milk
¼ cup sherry
4 ounces grated Cheddar cheese
1½ cups ground ham

1 clove garlic, pressed
1 teaspoon white pepper
Salt to taste
1 teaspoon onion juice
1 teaspoon oregano (optional)
12 ounces fine noodles
Parmesan cheese

Sauté mushrooms in butter. Add flour and gradually add half-and-half and milk to make a cream sauce. Add sherry, Cheddar cheese, ham, garlic, pepper, salt, onion juice, and oregano. Cook until smooth. Cook noodles in boiling water until tender; drain. Combine noodles and sauce; place in a 2½-quart casserole and top generously with Parmesan cheese. This may be prepared several hours earlier. Warm thoroughly in a 350° oven.

FISH AND SHELLFISH

All recipes are for eight portions unless otherwise stated.

CRAB OR SHRIMP MORNAY

1 stick butter
½ cup flour
¼ cup grated onions
½ cup chopped green onions
⅛ cup chopped parsley
2 cups heavy cream
1 cup dry white wine
2½ teaspoons salt
½ teaspoon white pepper
¼ teaspoon cayenne
2½ ounces imported Swiss cheese, minced

8 fresh artichokes, boiled, leaves scraped, bottoms quartered
2 tablespoons lemon juice
2 pounds lump crabmeat or 3 pounds shrimp, boiled and peeled
½ pound fresh mushrooms, sliced thickly
3 tablespoons Romano cheese

In 2-quart saucepan melt butter, stir in flour and cook 5 minutes over medium flame, stirring often. Add onions, green onions, and cook 2–3 minutes without browning. Stir in parsley, gradually add cream and allow to get hot, then add wine, salt, white pepper, cayenne. Blend well and bring to a simmer, stirring occasionally. Add Swiss cheese, stir, cover, turn off fire, and allow to cool. When sauce has cooled to lukewarm, stir in scrappings from artichoke leaves and lemon juice.

In a 3-quart casserole, make alternate layers of crabmeat, quartered artichoke bottoms, sliced raw mushrooms, using sauce between layers and on top. Sprinkle Romano cheese over the top, cover, and refrigerate until ready to reheat. Put uncovered, room temperature, casserole into a 350° oven and heat 30–45 minutes. If top is not browned, turn oven up to broil and brown top for 3–5 minutes. This is better made ahead of time. It is very rich and needs only a green salad and French bread served with it.

STUFFED CRABS

3 sticks butter
1 cup finely chopped green pepper
1 cup finely chopped green onions
½ cup finely chopped white onions
2 small garlic cloves, minced
¼ teaspoon thyme
1 bay leaf
1 cup finely chopped celery
7 ounces French bread rolls
   (pistolettes)

2 cups milk
4 teaspoons salt
1 teaspoon black pepper
¼ teaspoon cayenne
3 pounds crabmeat (1 pound claw
   and 2 pounds white meat) all
   well picked
Paprika
Buttered bread crumbs

In a large frying pan or Dutch oven, melt 2 sticks of butter and sauté green pepper, green onions, and white onions for 5 minutes. Add garlic, thyme, and bay leaf, sautéing slowly for about 30 minutes, or until soft. Add other stick of butter and celery and sauté for 5 minutes. Break French bread rolls into little pieces and soak well with milk. Add bread to seasonings and mix well, cooking over medium heat for 5 minutes. Add salt, black pepper, cayenne, and mix well. Add crabmeat, mixing thoroughly. Remove bay leaf and arrange crab mixture in individual shells. It is optional to top with paprika or buttered bread crumbs. Heat in a 400° oven only until hot. Plenty for 8—and some to freeze!

AVERY ISLAND TROUT

8–12 trout fillets (allow ⅓ pound
   per person)
Milk to cover (flavored with
   1 teaspoon salt and 6 drops
   Tabasco)
⅔ cup flour

2 sticks butter
½ teaspoon Tabasco
½ cup finely chopped green onions
½ cup finely chopped green pepper
⅔ cup dry white wine

Soak fillets 1 hour in flavored milk to cover. Dry fish well and salt generously on both sides. Dredge in flour and shake off excess. Put one stick of butter and Tabasco in baking dish (not aluminum), large enough to hold fillets without crowding. Place pan on middle shelf in broiler and let butter start to bubble. Remove from oven and sprinkle green onions and green pepper in bottom of pan, laying fillets on top. Use remaining butter to dot tops, and return to broiler. Cook 15–20 minutes (depending on size of fillets), basting twice. When fish are done and browned on top, remove them with a spatula to a heated serving platter and keep warm. Add wine to pan juices and place pan over a medium flame on top of range. Allow sauce to bubble rapidly, stirring constantly for 3–4 minutes. Spoon some sauce over trout and serve the rest in a heated sauceboat.

FRIED TROUT

8–12 trout fillets (⅓ pound per person) *	2 cups fine French bread crumbs
Milk to cover	1½ sticks butter
Salt	3 tablespoons oil
4–6 drops Tabasco	¼ cup chopped parsley
White pepper	Optional: 3–4 lemons, cut in wedges
3 eggs, beaten	

Soak fillets about 1 hour in milk, to which you have added 1 teaspoon salt and Tabasco. Remove fish and pat dry. Generously salt and pepper them; dip in eggs, then roll in bread crumbs. Melt 1 stick butter in a skillet and add 2 tablespoons oil. When mixture is very hot, add fillets, one at a time. Cook a few at a time, being sure not to overcrowd. Each one should sizzle loudly as it is put in. Allow grease to get hot between each addition. Brown on both sides. This takes about 5–7 minutes, depending on size of fillets. When cooked, remove to a heated serving platter and keep warm. When necessary to keep butter foaming over edges of fillets, add additional butter and oil to skillet. To serve, sprinkle with parsley and serve immediately. May be served plain with lemon wedges, or with one of the following sauces, passed separately in heated sauceboat.

SAUCE VERT:

¾ cup chopped green onions, including tops	⅛ teaspoon thyme
3 cloves chopped garlic	¾ teaspoon salt
¾ cup chopped celery	¼ teaspoon pepper
½ cup chopped parsley	2 sticks butter
	1 cup dry white wine

In a saucepan, sauté green onions, garlic, celery, parsley, thyme, salt, and pepper in butter for 30 minutes, stirring occasionally. Add wine, and simmer slowly 30 minutes. Purée in blender, then return to saucepan. Cover until ready to reheat.

SAUCE AUX CHEVRETTES:

2 pounds shrimp (heads and
    shells on)
2 cups dry vermouth
2 teaspoons salt
½ teaspoon white pepper
½ teaspoon cayenne pepper

3 cups finely chopped yellow
    onions
1 teaspoon garlic, minced
2 sticks butter
¼ cup flour
½ pint sour cream

Boil shrimp in vermouth, salt, white pepper, and cayenne until they turn pink—about 3 minutes. Drain—and reserve stock. Sauté onions and garlic slowly in butter on low fire until very clear—about 30 to 40 minutes. Add flour, and cook 5 minutes, stirring, to make a white roux. Add heated shrimp stock gradually, and simmer about 10 minutes, to make a medium-thick white sauce. Cover and allow to cool to lukewarm, add peeled shrimp, cover, and refrigerate. At serving time, add ½ pint sour cream, heat—*do not boil*—and serve with fried trout.

* Buster crabs may be used, allowing 3 per person, or soft-shell crabs, allowing 2 per person.

REDFISH COURT BOUILLON

4 dozen oysters, drained
6-pound redfish or red snapper,
    whole cleaned and scaled
Salt
White pepper
1 stick butter

1 lemon, sliced in 8 pieces
4 cups Creole sauce (see index)
40 medium shrimp, raw and
    peeled
2 teaspoons grated lemon rind
6 cups cooked rice

Drain oysters in a colander and run cold water over them for 1 minute. Wash and dry whole, cleaned fish and sprinkle generously with salt and white pepper, inside and out. Place in shallow baking pan. Put slices of lemon and butter underneath fish, in cavity and all over the top. If necessary to make fish fit pan, cut off tail or head or both and place in pan beside fish. These can be replaced on serving platter with parsley used to disguise cuts. Cook fish in 350° oven 13 minutes per pound.

When fish is half done, pour heated Creole sauce over top and continue cooking until it is within 15 minutes of being done. At this point, check fish at the thickest part to be sure that in 15 minutes all will be white with no pink or translucent part and that it will flake easily and that the flesh will lift cleanly from the bones. Cooking time will vary with the type of fish used. If you feel it needs more than 15 minutes, add cooking time at this point—not after adding seafood.

With 15 minutes cooking time left, add shrimp and oysters around sides of fish, sprinkle all with lemon rind, baste, and return to oven. Baste and stir once or twice to ensure that seafood cooks evenly. At the end of this time, being sure shrimp and oysters are done, remove fish from oven and lift with spatulas onto a heated serving platter. With slotted spoon, place seafood around sides and spoon some sauce over all. Garnish with parsley. Serve rest of sauce in heated sauceboat.

Cut portions of fish from top half beginning just behind head and trying to cut away and push aside row of bones along the upper and lower parts of fish. Place each portion on top of rice. Spoon shrimp, oysters, and sauce over all. When center bone is exposed, remove it and serve meat from bottom half of fish.

BAKED STUFFED FISH
WITH BROWN OYSTER SAUCE

FISH:

6 pounds will serve eight (redfish or red snapper)	1 lemon, sliced
	6 tablespoons butter
6 dozen oysters, drained	¼ cup chopped parsley

STUFFING:

5 cups crumbled unsweetened yellow cornbread (see index)	1 teaspoon salt
	¼ teaspoon pepper
1½ cups finely chopped green onions and tops	½ cup finely chopped parsley
	¼ teaspoon cayenne
2 cloves garlic, minced	⅛ teaspoon thyme
½ cup finely chopped green pepper	½ cup chicken stock
1 cup finely chopped celery	¼ cup cognac
2 sticks butter	

Sauté green onions, garlic, green pepper, and celery in butter until tender—about 20 minutes. Remove from fire, add salt, pepper, parsley, cayenne, thyme; stir, cover, and refrigerate. May be prepared a day ahead to this point. Heat sautéed vegetables and stir in very finely crumbled cornbread. Add chicken stock and cognac and blend well.

SAUCE:

1 stick butter
¼ cup flour
1 cup minced onions
1 bay leaf
1 teaspoon salt
½ teaspoon pepper

2 cups liquid:
1 cup dry white wine, plus
½ cup clam juice, plus ½ cup
water or: 1 cup clam juice plus
1 cup water
2 teaspoons grated lemon rind
2 tablespoons lemon juice
1 teaspoon Tabasco

Make dark brown roux with butter and flour. Add onions, bay leaf, salt, pepper, and liquid. Bring to a boil, then reduce heat, and simmer, partially covered, for ½ hour, stirring occasionally. Cover and refrigerate. When ready to use, heat and add lemon rind, lemon juice, Tabasco, and mix well. May be made a day ahead.

Drain oysters in a colander and run cold water over them for 1 minute. Wash and dry whole, cleaned fish. Sprinkle generously, inside and out, with salt and white pepper and place in shallow baking pan. Stuff cavity lightly with stuffing and tie string around fish in several places. Place slices of lemon down center of fish and dot with butter on top and also underneath (using 6 tablespoons). If necessary to make fish fit pan, cut off tail, or head or both and place in pan beside fish. These can be replaced on serving platter with parsley used to disguise cuts.

With remaining dressing, make 8 molds using a cup to make them firmly packed and uniform. Place them in separate baking dish and put in oven with fish during last 20 minutes of cooking time. Cook fish in 350° oven 12 minutes per pound. When fish is half done, pour heated sauce over it and continue to cook until it is within 10 minutes of being done. At this point, check fish at its thickest part to be sure that in 10 minutes it will all be white with no pink or translucent places, it will flake easily, and the flesh will lift cleanly from the bones. Cooking time will vary with the type fish used. If you feel it needs more than 10 minutes, add cooking time at this point, not after you have added the oysters. With 10 minutes left to cook fish, add oysters around the sides of fish.

Sprinkle all with parsley, baste, and return to oven. Using spatula and trussing strings, lift fish to a heated serving platter and remove strings. Surround it with dressing molds and use a slotted spoon to place oysters on top of fish and around sides. Keep fish warm. Place baking pan over high flame and boil sauce several minutes to thicken, stirring constantly. Spoon some sauce over fish and serve the remainder in a heated sauceboat. Garnish platter with parsley, put a pimento into eye, and place slices of lemon down center of fish.

To serve: cut first portion just behind head and only as deep as the center bone. Continue serving from top half of fish trying to cut away and push aside, the row of bones along the upper and lower parts of the fish. When center bone is exposed, remove it and serve meat from bottom half of fish. Place a dressing mold beside each piece of fish and spoon oysters and sauce over all.

TROUT VÉRONIQUE

½ cup coarsely chopped green
   onions
4 ribs celery, cut in strips
2 sprigs parsley
Salt to taste
White pepper to taste
8–12 trout fillets (allow ⅓ pound
   per person)
Cayenne to taste

2 cups dry white wine
2 cups water
4 egg yolks
1½ cups heavy cream
½ cup heavy cream, lightly
   whipped
1 stick butter
½ cup flour
48 white seedless grapes, halved

When preparing this dish, do not use aluminum cookware.

Spread green onions, celery, and parsley in the bottom of a shallow baking dish. Salt and pepper fillets well on both sides and sprinkle lightly with cayenne; arrange in a single layer on top of chopped seasonings. Heat wine and water together and add to baking dish. Cover fillets with buttered wax paper, cut to fit inside dish, making a hole in center of paper. Bake on lower rack of 350° oven for 8–10 minutes or until fish flakes when tested with a fork. Do not overcook. Transfer fillets to a warm ovenproof serving platter. Cover and keep warm.

Transfer poaching liquid and seasonings to a 2-quart saucepan; boil rapidly until it is reduced to 2 cups, approximately 20 minutes. Strain through cheesecloth. Beat egg yolks and mix with 1½ cups cream. Blend butter and flour in a heavy 3-quart saucepan for 3 minutes but do not brown. Gradually add reduced stock, stirring constantly with a whisk. Cook and stir over medium heat for 5 minutes until very thick.

Remove sauce from heat. Dribble 1 cup sauce into egg mixture, stirring vigorously with a whisk. Slowly add egg mixture to sauce beating with a whisk. Cook and stir sauce constantly over low heat until thickened, about 10 minutes. Remove from heat, correct seasoning and cover. This much may be done several hours ahead. When ready to serve heat sauce; do not boil. Blend in whipped cream. Dot tops of fillets with grapes and cover with sauce. Place in 325° oven only until heated through, then gratiné under a medium broiler to form a light brown crust. Serve immediately.

A variation of this is Trout Dugléré. Substitute 1½ cups small pieces of peeled, cored, seeded tomatoes for the grapes.

TROUT MEUNIÈRE or AMANDINE

8–12 trout fillets* (allow ⅓
   pound per person)
Milk to cover
2 teaspoons salt
4 drops Tabasco

1½ cups flour
1 teaspoon white pepper
1 stick butter
2 tablespoons oil

SAUCE:

2 sticks butter
½ cup sliced almonds (optional)
2 tablespoons lemon juice

2 teaspoons Worcestershire sauce
1 teaspoon salt
¼ cup chopped parsley

Soak fillets in a mixture of milk, 1 teaspoon salt, and Tabasco for at least 30 minutes. Season flour with 1 teaspoon salt and white pepper. Remove fillets from milk, pat dry, coat lightly with seasoned flour, shaking off excess. In a saucepan, melt 1 stick butter and add oil. In a large skillet, pour butter mixture to a depth of ⅛ inch. When grease is very hot, fry fillets, a few at a time, turning once. Cooking time will depend on size of fillets. Do not crowd fillets. Keep grease very hot and at proper depth by adding more from saucepan as necessary. Place cooked fillets on a warm platter and keep hot. When all are cooked, empty skillet and wipe out any burned flour.

Prepare sauce in same skillet by melting 2 sticks butter and lightly browning almonds. Add lemon juice, Worcestershire, salt, and parsley. Mix and heat well. Just before serving, pour some sauce over fillets and serve remaining portion in sauceboat.

* Buster crabs may be used, allowing 3 per person, or soft-shell crabs, allowing 2 per person.

WHOLE POACHED FISH (COLD)

FISH:

> *One large fish (about 12 pounds) or two small fish (6 pounds each) or small fish to equal 12 pounds. (Blackfish, redfish, red snapper, sheepshead, trout, etc. Any good eating fish, whole, cleaned, and scaled.)*

COURT BOUILLON:

3 quarts water	4 stalks celery and leaves
3 cups dry white wine	6 sprigs parsley
4 tablespoons salt	1 teaspoon thyme
2 carrots (sliced)	8 green onions (chopped)
1 onion (sliced)	3 lemons or limes (quartered,
40 peppercorns, bruised	squeezed, including rind)
8 cloves	4 garlic cloves, crushed
3 bay leaves	⅛ teaspoon cayenne pepper

Make court bouillon in fish poacher or roasting pan, and simmer, covered, for 30 minutes.

Wash and dry fish, sprinkle inside and out with salt and white pepper. If necessary, to make fish fit pan, cut off head and tail and place in cavity of fish. Wrap in cheesecloth and secure with string. Place in court bouillon, cover and simmer very slowly, 6 to 8 minutes per pound. Turn once if court bouillon doesn't cover fish. When using several small fish, figure the time for the individual fish sizes, not the total weight. When done, the fish should flake easily and flesh should lift cleanly from bones.

Lift fish out of liquid and place on flat pan. Remove cheesecloth. Allow to cool enough to handle. Remove skin and row of bones along top and bottom, and any dark meat of fish. Position head and tail on serving platter. Lift flesh from top half of fish and slide onto a piece of foil, then invert on platter between head and tail. Remove center bones from fish on cheese- cloth and check thoroughly for other bones in both halves. Using ends of cheesecloth, lift bottom half and place on top of other one on platter. Remove all skin and dark meat. Mold into fish shape with fingers and refrigerate. Discard all skin, place bones in court bouillon, and boil liquid down to two cups. Strain and refrigerate. If using two 6-pound fish, use one head and tail on platter and stack the flesh to form a very fat fish (4 fillets on top of each other) and proceed.

When court bouillon has jelled to a thick consistency, spoon over entire fish. Refrigerate. Just before serving, cover thickly with sauce, decorate with parsley to cover separation marks at head and tail. Place radishes in eyes and a row of overlapping slices of lemon and hard-boiled egg down the center. Garnish platter with lettuce, cucumbers, tomatoes, olives, pimentos, stuffed eggs, etc. Serve extra sauce on the side.

SAUCE I:

3 cups homemade mayonnaise
6 drops Tabasco
4 tablespoons lemon juice

½ cup capers and 1 teaspoon
   their liquid
2 tablespoons dry mustard or
4 tablespoons dijon mustard

SAUCE II:

Fish may be served with a sauce made of 3 cups sour cream, and seasoned to taste with salt and a generous amount of horse-radish. Serve garnished with fresh grapefruit sections and lettuce.

BAR-B-CUED SHRIMP

8–10 pounds jumbo shrimp, heads and shells on (20 shrimp per pound)

SAUCE:

1 pound butter
1 pound margarine
6 ounces Worcestershire sauce
8 tablespoons finely ground black
* pepper*

1 teaspoon ground rosemary
4 lemons, sliced
1 teaspoon Tabasco
4 teaspoon salt
2–4 cloves garlic (optional)

In a saucepan melt butter and margerine. Add Worcestershire, pepper, rosemary, lemon slices, Tabasco, salt, garlic and mix thoroughly. Divide shrimp between two large shallow pans and pour heated sauce over each. Stir well. Cook in a 400° oven about 15–20 minutes, turning once. Shells should be pink, the meat white and not translucent.

SHRIMP CREOLE

¼ cup flour
¼ cup bacon grease
2 cups chopped onions
½ cup chopped green onions
2 cloves garlic, minced
1 cup chopped green pepper
1 cup chopped celery, with leaves
1 teaspoon thyme
2 bay leaves
3 teaspoons salt
½ teaspoon pepper
6 ounces tomato paste

1 16-ounce can tomatoes, coarsely
* chopped, and liquid*
8 ounces tomato sauce
1 cup stock (made from boiling
* shrimp heads and shells), or*
* 1 cup water*
4 pounds peeled, deveined, raw
* shrimp*
1 teaspoon Tabasco
½ cup chopped parsley
1 tablespoon lemon juice
2 cups cooked rice

In a 4-quart Dutch oven, make a dark brown roux of flour and bacon grease. Add onions, green onions, garlic, green pepper, celery, thyme, bay leaf, salt, and pepper, and sauté, uncovered, over medium fire until onions are transparent and soft, about 30 minutes. Add tomato paste, and sauté 3 minutes. Add tomatoes, tomato sauce, stock (or water). Simmer very slowly, partially covered, for 1 hour, stirring occasionally. Add shrimp and cook until shrimp are just done, about 5 minutes. Add Tabasco, parsley, and lemon juice. Stir, cover, and remove from heat. Serve over rice.

This dish is best when allowed to stand several hours or overnight. Let cool and refrigerate. It also freezes well.

Remove from refrigerator 1 hour before serving. Heat quickly, without boiling, and serve immediately.

CRAWFISH ÉTOUFFÉ

2 sticks butter or 1½ sticks
   butter and ½ cup crawfish fat
¼ cup flour
1 cup chopped green onions
1 cup chopped yellow onions
2 garlic cloves, minced
½ cup chopped green pepper
½ cup chopped celery
1 bay leaf
¼ teaspoon thyme
½ to 1 teaspoon basil (optional)
8 ounces tomato sauce

½ teaspoon white pepper
2 teaspoons salt
1 tablespoon Worcestershire
Tabasco to taste
2 cups liquid*
2 pounds cooked crawfish tails
1 tablespoon lemon juice
1 tablespoon grated lemon rind
¼ cup minced parsley
2 tablespoons cognac (optional)
½ cup chopped green onion tops
   (optional)

Make a walnut-colored roux with 1 stick butter and flour. Add green onions, yellow onions, garlic, green pepper, celery, bay leaf, thyme, basil, and the remaining butter and crawfish fat. Sauté, uncovered, over medium flame for 30 minutes. Add tomato sauce, white pepper, salt, Worcestershire, Tabasco, and liquid. Bring to a boil, reduce heat and simmer slowly, uncovered, for 1 hour, stirring occasionally. Turn off fire. Add crawfish tails (if frozen, do not thaw), lemon juice, lemon rind, parsley, and cognac if desired. This is better made the day before or early in the morning. Cover and refrigerate. Remove from refrigerator 1 hour before serving. Heat quickly, without boiling, and serve immediately over steamed rice or in ramekins with French bread. If desired, garnish with raw green onion tops. It is recommended that if you use wine and/or cognac you omit the raw green onion tops.

* Liquid should be one of the following:
1 cup dry white wine plus ½ cup clam juice and ½ cup water or
1 cup clam juice plus 1 cup water or
2 cups water.

CRÊPES de la MER

½ cup flour
1½ sticks butter
1 cup chopped green onions
2 teaspoons garlic, minced
2 tablespoons tomato paste
1½–3 teaspoons curry powder
  (optional)
2½ teaspoons salt
½ teaspoon white pepper
1 cup liquid:
  1 cup shrimp stock (made by
  boiling heads and shells
  ½ hour) or: cup clam juice
  plus ½ cup water

1½ cups heavy cream
3 pounds small shrimp or
  2 pounds crabmeat or
  combination of the two
¼ cup lemon juice
3 cups sliced fresh mushrooms
⅓ cup minced parsley
1 teaspoon Tabasco
½ cup heavy cream, lightly
  whipped
16 6" crêpes (see index)

Lightly brown flour in 1 stick butter. Add onions and garlic, and cook until wilted (about 5 minutes). Add tomato paste, and cook 5 minutes. Add curry powder, salt, white pepper, stock, and 1½ cups cream. Bring to a boil. Add shrimp. Reduce heat and cook them slowly until they turn pink, 3–5 minutes. Remove from heat. (When using crabmeat, do not cook it, just stir it into sauce after sauce has simmered 3 minutes.) In a 12" skillet, melt remainder of butter, add 1 teaspoon lemon juice, mushrooms, and stir. Sauté them until the water from mushrooms has evaporated (about 5–7 minutes), then add them to the sauce along with remaining lemon juice, parsley and Tabasco. With slotted spoon, place some of mixture in the middle of a crêpe and fold two sides toward the center. Place in a shallow baking/serving dish approximately 9 x 13 x 2") with folded edges on bottom (to hold filling). You may use individual ramekins, allowing 2 crêpes for each one. Reserve extra sauce. This much may be done ahead. Cover and refrigerate. When ready to serve, bring crêpes to room temperature, mix lightly whipped cream with remaining sauce, and spoon generously over them. Cook on middle shelf in a 325° oven only until heated through, then gratiné under a medium broiler to form a light brown crust.

TIMBALES WITH MUSHROOM SAUCE

2 tablespoons butter
2 tablespoons flour
1½ teaspoons salt
¾ teaspoon white pepper
1½ teaspoons lemon rind
2 tablespoons ketchup
1½ teaspoons horse-radish
½ cup grated onions

2¼ cups heavy cream
6 egg yolks, beaten
⅓ cup dry white wine
2½ cups shrimp,* cooked and
  minced
3 egg whites, beaten
½ cup chopped water cress or
  chopped parsley

Melt butter and blend in flour. Cook over low flame for 2 minutes, stirring constantly. Remove from heat, and add salt, white pepper, lemon rind, ketchup, horse-radish, onions, cream, beaten egg yolks, wine, and shrimp. Put 3 quarts of water on range to boil. Beat egg whites until they stand in soft peaks, and fold them into mixture. Spoon mixture into 8 to 10 *heavily* buttered individual molds, 6–8 ounces each. Set them in a baking pan and pour in boiling water to reach halfway up sides of molds. Set timbales on middle rack of 300° oven and cook 40–50 minutes. Check for doneness by inserting a knife in center to see if custard is set and does not coat the blade. When done, remove molds from pan of water, run a knife around edge of each mold, and unmold onto heated serving platter. Sprinkle with water cress or parsley and serve with mushroom sauce (below) passed separately.

MUSHROOM SAUCE:

1½ sticks butter
1 tablespoon lemon juice
12 ounces fresh mushrooms, sliced
3 garlic cloves, whole but crushed
3 bay leaves
¼ cup flour

1¼ cups chicken or vegetable
  stock
½ cup heavy cream
¼ cup cognac
½ teaspoon salt
¼ teaspoon white pepper
½ teaspoon Tabasco

In a skillet melt 1 stick butter; add lemon juice and mushrooms, and stir. Add garlic and bay leaves; sauté 10 minutes. In a separate skillet, over a low fire, stir remaining butter and flour together for 5 minutes. To this roux

*You may substitute a great variety of cooked foods such as: lobster, broccoli, turkey, chicken, fish, crabmeat, ham, etc.

gradually add stock, cream, cognac, salt, and pepper. Simmer slowly uncovered for 5 minutes. Discard bay leaves and garlic. Stir in mushrooms, their liquid, and add Tabasco to the sauce. Cover and refrigerate until ready to reheat and serve.

STUFFED EGGPLANT

4 medium eggplant
Salted water to cover
1 cup chopped onions
1 cup chopped green onions
4 to 6 cloves garlic, minced
1 cup chopped green pepper
½ cup chopped celery
2 bay leaves
1 teaspoon thyme
4 teaspoons salt
½ teaspoon black pepper
4 tablespoons bacon grease

1½ pounds raw shrimp, peeled (if large shrimp, cut in ½" pieces)
1 stick butter
½ teaspoon Tabasco
1 tablespoon Worcestershire sauce
5 slices bread, crumbled
2 eggs, beaten
¼ cup chopped parsley
1 pound crabmeat
4 tablespoons lemon juice
8 tablespoons grated Romano cheese

Wash eggplant, cut off stems, cut in half, and boil in salted water about ten minutes or until tender. Scoop out insides and chop finely. Place shells in shallow baking dish. In a Dutch oven, sauté onions, green onions, garlic, green pepper, celery, bay leaves, thyme, salt, and pepper in bacon grease 20 minutes. Add chopped eggplant, and cook, covered, stirring occasionally for 30 minutes. In separate skillet, sauté shrimp in butter until they turn pink, about 1–2 minutes, then add to eggplant mixture. Mix Tabasco, Worcestershire sauce, bread, and eggs together; add to eggplant mixture. Stir in parsley, crabmeat, lemon juice, and blend all well. Remove bay leaves. Fill eggplant shells with mixture. Sprinkle each with 1 tablespoon Romano cheese and bake at 350° until hot and browned on top, about 30 to 40 minutes.

JAMBALAYA

½ pound chaurice (hot link sausage) or ½ pound smoked sausage, but then increase bacon grease to 4 tablespoons
Do not *sauté smoked sausage*
3 tablespoons bacon grease
½ pound ham, minced
1 cup chopped yellow onions
1 cup chopped green onions
1 cup chopped green pepper
3 garlic cloves, minced
1 bay leaf
½ teaspoon thyme
2 cups long-grain rice (washed, drained, but uncooked)

2 tablespoons tomato paste
2 cups chopped tomatoes (drain and reserve liquid)
½ cup chopped celery
¼ cup chopped parsley
2 teaspoons salt
½ teaspoon black pepper
Cayenne to taste (optional)
3 cups liquid from tomatoes and oysters
3 pounds cleaned raw shrimp
1 quart oysters (drain and reserve liquor)

In a 4-quart heavy pot, sauté sausage until firm, and remove with slotted spoon. Add bacon grease to drippings and sauté ham for 3 minutes. Add onions, green onions, green pepper, garlic, bay leaf, thyme, and sauté 5 minutes. Add rice, and sauté 3 minutes, stirring constantly; add tomato paste, and cook 3 minutes. Add sausage, tomatoes, celery, parsley, salt, pepper, and liquid. Bring to a boil, reduce heat, and cook slowly, covered, stirring occasionally until rice is done. About 12–15 minutes.

Transfer to a shallow 4-quart baking dish, and stir in seafood. Place uncovered in a preheated 350° oven and cook until seafood is done—20–30 minutes. Stir twice while baking using a large fork to fluff the rice and ensure the seafood cooking evenly.

OYSTERS EN BROCHETTE

SAUCE:

2 sticks butter
4–5 tablespoons lemon juice
2 teaspoons Tabasco

2 teaspoons salt
1½ tablespoons Worcestershire sauce (optional)

Melt butter; add lemon juice, Tabasco, salt, and Worcestershire sauce and set aside.

8 dozen oysters	*Flour*
24 pieces bacon	*½ cup finely chopped water cress*
24 fresh mushroom caps (optional)	*or parsley*
Salt	*24 cherry tomatoes (optional)*
Freshly ground black pepper	*Toasted French bread*

Drain oysters. Cut bacon into 1½" pieces and partially cook to remove some grease. On skewers, alternate bacon, oysters, mushrooms, and tomatoes, beginning and ending with bacon. Generously sprinkle with salt and pepper on both sides. Sprinkle with flour, shaking off excess. Place skewers in a shallow pan and brush sauce onto both sides. Place on center rack in broiler and cook 5 minutes on each side—basting when you turn. To serve; place toasted French bread on plate and slide contents of one skewer onto bread. Spoon sauce on top and sprinkle with chopped water cress.

OYSTERS AND ARTICHOKES IN A VOL-AU-VENT

A vol-au-vent is a large puff pastry shell with a top, and can be purchased from some bakeries. May also be served in individual pastry shells, or over toast.

2½ sticks butter	*2 tablespoons lemon juice*
6 tablespoons flour	*10 dozen small oysters, drained,*
1 cup finely chopped green onions	*reserve liquor*
2 garlic cloves, minced	*10 artichokes, boiled, leaves*
1 cup finely chopped celery	*scraped, bottoms put aside*
2 bay leaves	*1½ teaspoons Tabasco*
⅛ teaspoon thyme	*½ cup dry white wine*
1½ teaspoons salt	*A 4-quart vol-au-vent**
½ teaspoon pepper	*½ cup finely chopped parsley*
18 ounces sliced fresh mushrooms	

In a 4-quart Dutch oven, make a dark brown roux with 2 sticks butter and flour. Add green onions, garlic, celery, bay leaves, thyme, salt, and pepper, and cook until vegetables are tender, about 20 minutes, stirring occasionally.

In separate skillet, melt remaining ½ stick butter, add 1 teaspoon lemon juice, mushrooms, and stir. Sauté them until the water from mushrooms has evaporated (about 5 minutes). Drain oysters very well in a colander, and add their liquor to roux. Cook sauce, uncovered, 45 minutes, or until it is quite thick. Add mushrooms and artichoke scrapings, and place artichoke bottoms on top of roux. Cover and refrigerate until ready to use. Recipe may be done day ahead to this point.

When ready to complete, heat sauce slowly to prevent burning on bottom. Be careful not to break artichoke bottoms. Place oysters in a single layer in a shallow pan, and bake in 400° oven for 5–6 minutes, or until *just* curled. Remove artichoke bottoms from sauce and keep warm. With a slotted spoon, transfer oysters to heated sauce, then add wine, remainder of lemon juice, and Tabasco, stirring well. Remove bay leaves.

During this time, place vol-au-vent in a 400° oven, watching carefully. When brown and crispy on the outside, move to a heated serving platter. Remove top. Arrange artichoke bottoms in bottom of vol-au-vent, and pour in oyster mixture. Cover with pastry top, and garnish with chopped parsley. To serve: cut through the whole vol-au-vent with knife from top to bottom and, with aid of spatula, serve each portion as you would a pie.

* 16 individual pastry shells may be substituted.

OYSTERS AU SAUCE CRÈME

1 cup finely chopped green onions and tops	1–1½ cups dry sherry
1 pound butter	1½ teaspoons salt
1 pound sliced fresh mushrooms	½ teaspoon cayenne
¼ cup lemon juice	1¾ ounces anchovy paste
1 cup flour	8 dozen oysters
1 cup milk	10 ounces pimentos
1 cup heavy cream	¼ cup cognac

Sauté green onions in 1 stick of butter about 5 minutes, or until very tender. Add another stick of butter, 1 teaspoon lemon juice, mushrooms, and stir. Sauté them until the water from mushrooms has evaporated (about 5–7 minutes). In separate pan, make white roux with 2 sticks butter and flour. Cook on low fire, stirring, about 5 minutes. Gradually add milk, cream, sherry, salt, cayenne, anchovy paste, and cook 15 minutes over low fire, stirring often.

The sauce should be very thick because the oysters will water. Stir in green onions, mushrooms, and their butter. This sauce is better made ahead and refrigerated. When ready to complete, heat sauce. Drain oysters and place in a single layer in a shallow pan and bake in a 400° oven for about 5-6 minutes, or until *just* curled. With a slotted spoon, add them to the heated sauce along with the rest of the lemon juice, pimentos, and cognac. Heat quickly, without boiling, and serve immediately in patty shells or with toasted French bread or rolls. If sauce is too thick, add small amount of milk.

DEVILED OYSTERS

⅔ cup oil
⅔ cup flour
2 cups finely chopped onions
1 cup finely chopped green onions
2 cloves garlic, finely chopped
1½ cups finely chopped green
  pepper
1 cup finely chopped celery
1 bay leaf
¼ teaspoon thyme

3 cups fresh mushrooms, sliced
4 tablespoons lemon juice
1 stick butter
2 teaspoons salt
½ teaspoon black pepper
⅛ teaspoon cayenne pepper
2 tablespoons Worcestershire
  sauce
8 dozen small oysters
1¼ cups French bread crumbs

Make dark brown roux with oil and flour. Add onions, green onions, garlic, green pepper, celery, bay leaf, and thyme. Cook until very tender, about 45 minutes. In separate pan, melt butter, add 1 teaspoon lemon juice, mushrooms, and stir. Sauté them until the water from mushrooms has evaporated (about 5-7 minutes). Then add to the sauce. Season with salt, pepper, cayenne, Worcestershire. (This sauce is better done the day before.) When ready to serve, heat sauce. Drain oysters and place in a single layer in shallow pan and bake at 400° until just curled, about 5 to 6 minutes. Using a slotted spoon, transfer oysters to sauce. Add remaining lemon juice and bread crumbs. Blend well and pour into a shallow baking dish or into individual ramekins. Heat in 400° oven just until hot.

POULTRY AND GAME

All recipes are for eight portions unless otherwise stated.

CHICKEN DUXELLES

8 chicken breasts (wing attached)　　Freshly ground black pepper
2 tablespoons lemon juice　　½ stick butter
2 teaspoons thyme　　¼ cup madeira (optional)
Salt to taste

DUXELLES:

12 ounces fresh mushrooms, finely　　2 tablespoons finely chopped
　chopped　　　parsley
2 tablespoons butter　　Salt to taste
3 tablespoons finely chopped　　Pepper to taste
　onions

SAUCE:

Butter that remains in baking　　1½ cups whipping cream
　dish　　1 cup slivered almonds, toasted
2 tablespoons flour　　Garnish: parsley and paprika
1 beef bouillon cube

Prepare and season chicken at least 1 hour before cooking. Skin and debone breasts, removing 2 pinions but leaving main wing bone. Rub with lemon juice, thyme, salt, and pepper. Preheat oven to 400° and melt ½ stick butter in a large, shallow baking dish. Arrange breasts in a single layer; turn each breast once to coat with butter. Add madeira, cover lightly with wax paper; cook 10–12 minutes. Transfer chicken to warm serving dish, wing bone down. Reserve butter.

In a skillet prepare duxelles by combining mushrooms, butter, onions, parsley, salt, and pepper; cook until mushroom liquid disappears, approximately 10 minutes. Spoon duxelles onto chicken pieces equally. Keep warm while making sauce.

To original baking dish add 2 tablespoons flour; stir and cook 3 minutes without browning. Add bouillon cube and cream, and boil rapidly to thicken, stirring constantly. Spoon over chicken; top with almonds, parsley, and paprika. Serve.

CHICKEN DIJON

16 chicken pieces, boned	2 tablespoons Worcestershire
Salted milk*	sauce
1½ cups sour cream	3 teaspoons lemon juice
1 cup Dijon-type mustard	3 cloves garlic, pressed
3 teaspoons paprika	Pepper
2 teaspoons celery salt	1 cup fine cracker crumbs

Soak chicken pieces in salted milk 1 hour. In separate bowl, mix sour cream, mustard, paprika, celery salt, Worcestershire, lemon juice, and garlic. Let stand one hour. Dry chicken and sprinkle with pepper. Heavily coat chicken pieces with sour cream mixture, sprinkle with crumbs, and place on a greased rack in a shallow baking pan. Bake in 400° oven for 15 minutes, then lower oven temperature to 325° and continue baking for 20 minutes.

* For each ¼ cup milk add ¼ teaspoon salt.

CHICKEN CHASSEUR

2 broilers, quartered, or 16	1 teaspoon thyme
pieces of frying chicken	1 teaspoon salt
4 tablespoons cooking oil	1 teaspoon pepper
2½ cups chopped onions	¾ cup consommé
2 tablespoons flour	⅔ cup dry white wine
5 tablespoons tomato paste	¾ pound mushrooms, sliced
3 medium tomatoes, peeled,	2 tablespoons butter
seeded, and chopped	3 tablespoons chopped parsley
2 cloves garlic, pressed	8 slices French bread (½" thick)
2 bay leaves	fried in butter

Brown well-dried chicken in oil and place in a large covered pot to keep warm. Brown onions in same oil, then sprinkle flour over onion and continue cooking for 3 to 5 minutes, stirring constantly. Stir in tomato paste, tomatoes, garlic, bay leaves, thyme, salt, pepper, consommé, and wine. Bring to a boil, then pour over chicken. Cover tightly and bake in 350° oven until tender, about 30 to 45 minutes. In original pan, sauté mushrooms over low flame, adding butter if necessary. When chicken is tender, transfer to serving dish, using a slotted spoon. Add mushrooms to gravy and pour over chicken. Garnish with parsley and border dish with French bread. Remove bay leaves before serving.

CHICKEN HOLLANDAISE

8 breasts of chicken
1 stick butter
¾ cup brandy
1¼ cup button mushrooms
1 cup well-seasoned chicken stock
¾ cup white wine

Salt to taste
Pepper to taste
2 cups Hollandaise sauce
  (see index)
3 tablespoons chopped chives

Skin and debone chicken breasts. In a skillet, melt butter and brown chicken breasts on both sides. Heat brandy, ignite it, and pour over chicken. When flame dies down, add mushrooms, stock, wine, and simmer for 5 minutes. Season with salt and pepper. Transfer all to shallow baking dish and bake, uncovered, in a 250° oven for 1 hour. Before serving, spoon Hollandaise over chicken and garnish with chives.

CHICKEN WITH PEACHES

1½ cups orange juice
2½ cups sliced fresh peaches
3 tablespoons brown sugar
3 tablespoons white vinegar
1½ teaspoons nutmeg or mace
1½ teaspoons basil
2 cloves garlic, minced

16 selected pieces frying
  chicken, lightly salted
¾ cup flour mixed with
  2 teaspoons salt and
  ⅓ teaspoon black pepper
Cooking oil
Garnish: crabapples or fresh mint
  (optional)

In a pan prepare sauce by combining juice and peaches with sugar, vinegar, nutmeg (or mace), basil, and garlic. Simmer, tightly covered, for 10 minutes. Dredge dried and lightly salted chicken in seasoned flour. In a large, deep, heavy skillet pour cooking oil to ½″ depth, heat, and brown chicken well. Remove chicken from skillet and set aside on warm platter. Discard excess oil saving pan drippings; add ⅓ cup of liquid from sauce and stir well. Replace chicken in skillet and pour remaining sauce and fruit over chicken. Simmer covered for twenty minutes. Serve on hot platter garnished with crabapples or fresh mint.

CHICKEN REGINA

8 chicken breasts	1 cup whipping cream
Salt	1 cup light cream
White pepper	8 artichoke bottoms cooked and
2 tablespoons lemon juice	sliced
1 onion, quartered	2 egg yolks, beaten
1 cup dry white wine	8 thick slices of tomato
6 tablespoons butter	¼ cup chopped parsley
3 tablespoons flour	

Simmer breasts in water to cover adding salt, pepper, lemon juice, and onion. When fork tender, approximately 30 minutes, remove to platter, reserving broth. Combine 2 cups of broth with wine and, over medium flame, reduce to 2 cups and set aside. Prepare a sauce by melting 3 tablespoons butter and slowly add flour, blending well, but not browning. Add the 2 cups of wine-broth mixture and cook over low heat for 10 minutes, stirring constantly. Stir in ½ cup whipping cream, correct seasoning if necessary and set cream sauce aside. Skin and debone chicken, place in a saucepan, and add light cream. Cook over low heat until the cream is reduced by about ⅓ and then add 1 cup of cream sauce. Line the bottom of an ovenproof serving dish with artichoke bottoms, and cover with chicken and sauce. To the remaining cup of sauce, add the beaten egg yolks, stirring constantly over low heat and permit to thicken. Remove from heat and fold in ½ cup whipped cream. Pour this over the chicken and top with tomato slices which have been sprinkled with salt and pepper and broiled in 3 tablespoons butter. Brown casserole quickly in broiler, garnish with parsley, and serve immediately.

CHICKEN ROCHAMBEAU

⅔ cup finely chopped white onions
4 tablespoons butter
⅓ cup flour
4 cloves garlic, pressed
⅓ to ½ cup sugar
⅓ cup white vinegar
⅓ cup Worcestershire sauce
2 cups chicken stock
8 breast quarters of frying
   chicken, wing pinions removed

⅓ cup cooking oil
Flour
Salt
Pepper
8 slices cooked ham
8 slices dry toast
Béarnaise sauce (see index)
Garnish: water cress

To make gravy, sauté onions in butter until transparent. Blend in ⅓ cup flour and brown with onions. Add garlic, sugar, vinegar, Worcestershire, and stock, being careful to add stock slowly. Cook over low heat, stirring occasionally, for one hour. Gravy will be thick. Salt and pepper thoroughly dried chicken pieces and dust with flour; brown in oil over medium heat. Transfer to a baking dish and place in 250° oven to complete cooking, approximately 20–30 minutes, while preparing béarnaise sauce. Before serving, place ham on toast and spread 2 tablespoons of gravy over each slice of ham; add chicken and cover each serving with remaining gravy. Top each with béarnaise sauce and garnish with water cress.

COQ AU VIN

16 pieces frying chicken
Salt
Pepper
Flour
6 tablespoons butter
2 tablespoons oil
1 cup ham, preferably raw, diced
   and fat removed
16 small white onions, peeled

2 small cloves garlic, finely
   chopped
Bouquet garni of 3 sprigs
   parsley, 2 bay leaves, 2 sprigs
   thyme tied together
2½ ounces brandy
2½ cups claret or burgundy wine
8 ounces fresh mushrooms, sliced
Garnish: chopped parsley

Season chicken with salt and pepper; dredge in flour. In a large, non-aluminum Dutch oven combine 4 tablespoons butter with oil, and brown chicken. When chicken has browned, remove from Dutch oven temporarily. Place ham, onions, garlic, and bouquet garni in Dutch oven, and replace chicken. Heat brandy, ignite it, and pour over chicken. Add wine, and simmer, covered, until sauce thickens and chicken is tender—about 45 minutes to 1 hour. This much should be prepared a day ahead. Transfer to an ovenproof serving dish. To reheat, remove bouquet garni, correct seasoning, and place in 350° oven until thoroughly heated. While warming, sauté mushrooms in 2 tablespoons butter. When chicken is ready, stir in mushrooms; garnish with parsley and serve.

ROLLED CHICKEN SUPREMES

8 large chicken breasts
8 slices imported Swiss cheese
8 slices boiled ham
3 eggs

3 cups seasoned bread crumbs,
  rolled fine
1 stick butter

Debone breasts. Prepare Supremes by wrapping cheese and then ham around each breast. Secure well with wooden toothpicks. Beat eggs; dip each Supreme in egg and roll in bread crumbs. In shallow baking dish, melt one stick of butter and add Supremes. Place on low rack in 350° oven and bake 35 minutes, turning only once during cooking time. Baste often, adding more butter if necessary.

POULET MARENGO

8 chicken breasts
8 chicken thighs
Salt
Pepper
Flour
¼ cup olive oil
1 medium green pepper, cut in
  strips
4 tablespoons chopped green
  onions
4 cloves garlic, pressed

3 tablespoons finely chopped
  parsley
½ cup white wine
½ cup chicken stock
1 bay leaf
6 medium tomatoes, peeled, seeded
  and cut in strips
¾ cup ripe olives, halved
12 small white onions, peeled
⅛ teaspoon thyme
Parsley to garnish

Skin chicken, then wash and dry it; salt and pepper and lightly dust pieces with flour. In a skillet slowly brown chicken in olive oil over low flame, turning frequently. As chicken browns, transfer to a large covered baking dish. From skillet, pour off all but 1 tablespoon oil and add green pepper, green onions, and garlic. Cook slowly until tender. Add parsley, wine, stock, bay leaf, tomatoes, olives, onions, thyme, and 2 teaspoons salt. Mix and cook over low heat an additional 5 minutes. Pour sauce over chicken and bake covered in 325° oven approximately 45 minutes. Remove bay leaf and garnish with parsley.

CORNISH HENS—GRAPE COGNAC SAUCE

8 Cornish hens	½ cup finely chopped celery
Salt	½ pound mushrooms, sliced
Pepper	3 cups soft white bread crumbs
Soda	1 cup finely chopped parsley
½ cup finely chopped ham	1 teaspoon white pepper
1 stick butter	½ cup cognac
1 cup finely chopped onions	

Wash and dry hens; rub cavities with equal parts of salt, pepper, and soda. In a heavy skillet, sauté ham 3 to 4 minutes in 1 tablespoon butter. Remove ham and set aside. Add 3 tablespoons butter and sauté onion with celery for 10 minutes. Add mushrooms and cook an additional 10 minutes. Remove from fire and mix in bread crumbs, ham, parsley, and white pepper. Stuff birds, coat with remaining softened butter, salt, and pepper lightly and place in a shallow roasting pan. Sprinkle hens with ¼ cup cognac and bake in 350° oven for 45 minutes, brushing frequently with pan drippings and remaining cognac. Transfer hens, halved if desired, to a heated serving dish and keep warm while preparing sauce.

SAUCE:

2 pounds seedless grapes, halved	½ cup cognac
1 cup consommé	Salt
2 tablespoons butter	Pepper

To pan drippings, add grapes, consommé, butter, cognac, salt, pepper, and simmer until thoroughly heated. Serve over hens or in separate sauceboat.

CHICKEN LIVERS FINANCIÈRE

16 large green olives
6 tablespoons butter
½ cup minced green onions, bulb
   only
¾ cup madeira or ¾ cup beef stock
6 ounces sliced mushrooms

1½ cups brown sauce (see index)
¼ cup lemon juice
⅛ teaspoon cayenne
2 pounds chicken livers
¼ cup cognac (optional)

Cut olives lengthwise in strips and drop into boiling water to cover. Let stand 1 minute; drain and set aside. Melt 2 tablespoons butter in a skillet; add green onions, and sauté until transparent. Add madeira, and continue cooking until onions are dark. Stir in mushrooms, brown sauce, lemon juice, and cayenne. Cook 5 minutes, stirring constantly, and remove from fire. Can be prepared to this point several hours ahead. Clean, wash, dry, and lightly salt chicken livers. Sauté in 4 tablespoons butter for 5 minutes, or until lightly browned but still pink inside. Add warmed cognac and ignite dish. Transfer livers to a warm plate. To pan drippings add sauce and stir well. To serve, reheat sauce; add livers and olives and cook until piping hot. Serve immediately. Bite-size pieces of cooked chicken or turkey breast may be substituted for sautéed livers with great success.

ROAST TURKEY

10–12 pound turkey
   (room temperature)
Salt
2 teaspoons baking soda

Pepper
6 tablespoons butter
½ cup cognac

Wash and dry turkey. Rub body and neck cavities with mixture of 2 teaspoons salt, baking soda, and 1 teaspoon pepper. Rub exterior with 2 tablespoons of butter and sprinkle generously with salt and pepper. Lightly stuff cavities and truss. Fold wings under, put in roasting pan breast side up, and place in preheated 450° oven. Reduce heat immediately to 325° and cook stuffed bird uncovered for first hour, basting frequently with a combination of 4 tablespoons butter and ½ cup cognac. After 1 hour cover bird and cook an additional 2 hours, basting frequently. Remove cover and continue cooking until turkey has been cooked 20 minutes per pound. Remove from oven and let turkey sit 20 minutes before carving.

CORNBREAD STUFFING

1 cornbread recipe (see index)
Turkey neck
Gizzard
Liver
1 cup finely chopped green onions
1 cup finely chopped celery
½ cup finely chopped green pepper

½ stick butter
2 dozen oysters, drained and
   chopped
Salt to taste
Pepper to taste
Oyster liquor, stock, or milk

Make corn bread, omitting sugar if desired. Boil neck and gizzard in enough water to obtain ½ cup stock. Chop liver and gizzard when cool. In a large skillet, sauté green onions, celery, and green pepper in butter until soft and transparent. Add liver, gizzard, and oysters, stirring lightly for 1 or 2 minutes. Remove from fire and mix in crumbled cornbread. Salt and pepper to taste. Moisten to desired consistency with stock, oyster liquor, or milk. Stuff a 12–14 pound turkey lightly, and bake. Stuffing freezes well.

GROUND ARTICHOKE (JERUSALEM) STUFFING

(12-pound turkey)

5 pounds ground artichokes
1 turkey gizzard, chopped after
   boiling
1 stick butter
1 turkey liver, chopped raw
1 turkey heart, chopped raw
1 chopped green pepper
1 cup chopped celery
½ cup chopped celery leaves
½ cup chopped parsley
1 cup chopped onions

2 cloves finely chopped garlic
1 cup chopped green onions
1 bay leaf
1 sprig thyme
2 teaspoons salt
1 teaspoon pepper
6 slices bread (soaked in water)
1 tablespoon Worcestershire
   sauce
2 eggs, beaten

Parboil ground artichokes until just fork tender. Peel and finely chop. Boil gizzard, reserving water to moisten dressing. In 4 tablespoons butter, fry gizzard, liver, and heart. In remaining butter, sauté green pepper, celery, celery leaves, parsley, onions, garlic, green onions, and bay leaf. Add thyme, salt, pepper, and bread (which has been squeezed dry). Add gizzard mixture and artichokes, and fry about 5 minutes. Remove from fire, take out bay leaf; add Worcestershire and stir in eggs. Moisten to desired consistency with gizzard broth. When cool, stuff turkey and bake. Freezes well.

LOUISIANA YAM AND APPLE STUFFING

4 cups diced, peeled apples	1 stick butter
1 cup chopped celery	1 cup brown sugar
1 cup water	Salt
8 cups mashed yams	1 cup chopped pecans
2 tablespoons lemon juice	1 lemon rind grated
1 teaspoon cinnamon	

Simmer diced apples and celery in 1 cup water until just tender. Drain, reserving liquid. Meanwhile boil yams in water to cover, approximately 25 minutes. Peel yams and mash with lemon juice, cinnamon, butter, brown sugar, and salt. Use apple liquid to moisten. Add apple, celery, pecans, and grated lemon rind. Toss. Correct seasoning. Dressing is now ready for 2 ducklings, 2 capons, or a 12-pound turkey.

OYSTER AND PECAN STUFFING

3 loaves French bread for crumbs (8 ounces each)	2 pounds ground meat
	3 or 4 dozen oysters, drained, reserving liquor
1½ cups finely chopped green onions	1 cup chopped pecans
1½ cups finely chopped white onions	1 cup chopped parsley
	Salt to taste
4 cups finely chopped green pepper	Pepper to taste
	Cayenne pepper to taste
3 teaspoons minced garlic	1 bay leaf
1½ sticks butter	½ teaspoon thyme
5 cups finely chopped celery	2 eggs, beaten

Dry French bread in 250° oven and roll into fine crumbs. Sauté green onions, onions, green pepper, and garlic in 1 stick butter until transparent. Add celery, and sauté two additional minutes. In a separate skillet, fry ground meat until done, and drain. Chop oysters, if large. Mix meat, oysters, and sautéed vegetables together, and add bread crumbs. Add oyster liquor by the spoonful until stuffing has reached desired consistency. Add pecans, parsley, salt, pepper, cayenne, bay leaf, and thyme. Combine eggs with ½ stick softened butter and mix into stuffing. Lightly stuff 12–14 pound turkey.

GAME

All recipes are for eight portions unless otherwise stated.

Freshly shot birds are preferable to frozen ones. In preparing freshly picked or skinned birds, remove entrails and the two oil glands in the tail. On larger birds, singe remaining pinfeathers. Wash cavity with baking soda and water and rinse thoroughly. Reserve cleaned giblets and neck for making stock. The heart, liver and cleaned gizzard of the dove, or smaller bird are considered a special delicacy by many Louisianians.

Birds should be at room temperature before cooking. Drain cavity completely; dry bird well inside and out. The cooking time and degree of tenderness will depend on several factors: the size and age of the bird and whether the bird is fresh or has been frozen. Test bird for doneness by pricking meatiest part of the thigh with a fork—rosy juice indicates the meat is rare and clear juice indicates the meat is well done. As a general rule, game birds with darker meat, such as mallard, woodcock and dove, may be served rare or medium, while birds with whiter flesh, such as quail, are usually well done. Cooked game birds should be served immediately on warmed platters with appropriate garnish.

To freeze cleaned birds: submerge in water in empty milk cartons or plastic containers. Wrap giblets in freezer paper or plastic freezer bags and freeze. Birds kept in the freezer for longer than eight months tend to dry and, with the exception of duck destined for duck gumbo, should be used within an eight- or nine-month period.

GLAZED WILD DUCK

8 large ducks	*2 oranges, quartered*
Salt	*⅓ cup chopped onions*
Pepper	*2 cups chopped celery*
2 apples, quartered	*Garnish: parsley sprigs*

GLAZE:

2 cups currant jelly   6 tablespoons cornstarch
2 tablespoons lemon juice   3 tablespoons water
¼ teaspoon powdered ginger   ½ cup cognac
¼ teaspoon powdered cloves

Dry ducks. Salt and pepper inside and out. Stuff each cavity with a piece
of apple, a piece of orange, 2 teaspoons onion, and ¼ cup celery. Place ducks
in a single layer in a heavy roasting pan; add enough water to half cover
the ducks. Cover and cook in 325° oven for about 2 hours or until fork
tender. Prepare glaze. Slowly melt jelly in saucepan; add lemon juice, ginger,
and cloves. Mix cornstarch with water and add to pan. Stir constantly until
sauce becomes clear and thick. Glaze may be made to this point a day ahead
and refrigerated. When ducks are cooked, cut in half, discard stuffing, and
arrange on warm platter. Add cognac to glaze mixture and heat; spoon over
duck and garnish with parsley. Serve remaining glaze in heated sauceboat.

DOVES CHASSEUR

16 doves*   ⅔ cup liquid: water, consommé or
Salt   wine
Pepper   12 ounces mushrooms
Flour   2 tablespoons butter
8 slices bacon   1 teaspoon lemon juice
⅛ teaspoon Tabasco   Garnish: chopped parsley
4 tablespoons Worcestershire
    sauce

Dry, salt, and pepper doves well, inside and out. Dust lightly with flour.
In Dutch oven large enough for single layer of doves, cook bacon until crisp.
Remove, drain, and reserve. Brown doves on all sides in hot bacon grease.
With breast down, turn fire low, add Tabasco, Worcestershire, and ⅔ cup
liquid, cover and cook 20 minutes. Stir, turn doves breast up, continue
cooking covered for 20 minutes. Add more liquid if necessary. While doves
are cooking, sauté mushrooms lightly in butter and lemon juice. Add mushrooms to doves for last 15 minutes of cooking. Before serving, crumble bacon
over doves. Garnish with chopped parsley.

* Eight teals may be substituted.

DUCK SUPREMES

(Mallard, pintail, gray duck)

1½ sticks butter
1 cup finely chopped green onions
1 clove garlic, pressed
2 cups rice (long-grain and wild, mixed)
4 cups water
1 cup vermouth
1 cup finely chopped celery
1 bay leaf
½ teaspoon each: thyme, oregano sweet basil, sweet marjoram

2 teaspoons salt
¼ teaspoon white pepper
⅛ teaspoon cayenne
½ cup chopped parsley
16 duck supremes (skinless, boneless meat from each side of breast)
Salt, pepper
Flour
3 tablespoons cooking oil
½ cup cognac

In a large, heavy pot melt 1 stick butter, and sauté onions and garlic until transparent. Stir in rice, and cook 3 minutes. Add water and vermouth; stir in celery, bay leaf, thyme, oregano, sweet basil, sweet marjoram, 2 teaspoons salt, ¼ teaspoon white pepper, and ⅛ teaspoon cayenne. Remove from fire; stir in parsley and transfer all to a covered 4-quart baking dish. Place in 325° oven for 15 minutes. Lightly salt, pepper, and flour Supremes. In a heavy skillet sauté supremes very quickly in extremely hot oil until light brown on each side, to seal in juices. Remove Supremes and drain excess fat from pan. Melt remaining butter in pan and return Supremes. Warm cognac, ignite and pour over Supremes. Transfer Supremes to top of rice casserole and pour pan juices over all; cover and return to oven for 45 minutes.

DUCK WITH HERBS

8 large ducks
1 tablespoon marjoram
1 tablespoon sage
1 tablespoon thyme
1 tablespoon black pepper
1 tablespoon salt

4 oranges, quartered
4 onions, quartered
4 stalks celery, cut in pieces
3 tablespoons flour
1 tablespoon paprika
3 cups stock or consommé

Wash and dry ducks well. Rub each well with a mixture of marjoram, sage, thyme, black pepper, and salt. Stuff each duck with pieces of orange, onion, and celery. Place breast side down in an uncovered roasting pan, leaving space between each duck so they will brown. Sprinkle ducks with 1½ tablespoons flour and 1½ teaspoons paprika; bake in 450° oven for 30 minutes. Skim off grease, turn breast side up; sprinkle on remaining flour and paprika, and continue to bake for 30 minutes. Skim off grease and pour stock or consommé over ducks, mixing with scrapings from pan. Lower oven to 300°; return ducks, and cook, basting often, for 45 minutes or until they are tender. To serve, cut ducks in half and remove stuffing. Serve gravy from a sauceboat.

QUAIL IN WINE

16 quails	6 tablespoons diced green pepper
Salt	12 ounces mushrooms (stems
Pepper	removed but reserved)
1¾ sticks butter	2 tablespoons flour
1½ cups diced carrots	3 cups chicken stock
6 tablespoons diced onions	2 cups dry white wine

Sprinkle quails inside and out with salt and pepper. In a heavy skillet melt 8 tablespoons butter and cook quails until golden brown on all sides. When browning birds be careful not to puncture bodies. Grease a 4-quart covered casserole with 2 tablespoons butter and arrange quails breast side up; set aside. To original skillet add carrots, onions, green pepper, and mushroom stems; cook slowly, stirring frequently for 5 minutes. Blend in flour, mixing well; add stock, stirring approximately 10 minutes or until sauce has thickened. Add salt and pepper to taste and continue to simmer, stirring occasionally for 10 minutes. While sauce is simmering pour wine over quail and bake in 350° oven for 15 minutes, basting frequently to keep birds from drying out. Strain vegetable sauce over quail, mashing vegetables against strainer to release all juices; discard vegetables. Turn quail breast side down and cook covered an additional 45 minutes until tender. Sauté mushroom caps in 4 tablespoons butter until tender and set aside. Transfer quail to hot platter, breast side up. Garnish platter with sautéed mushroom caps. Serve remaining sauce in a sauceboat.

ROAST DUCK WITH SHADOWS-ON-THE-TECHE SAUCE

8 large ducks or 8 teals
Salt
Pepper
2 medium onions, peeled and
    quartered

2 apples, cored and quartered
4 stalks celery, cut in pieces
½ cup butter, melted

Dry, salt, and pepper duck inside and out. Stuff each cavity with a piece of onion, apple, and celery. Place in a large roasting pan, leaving space between each duck. Roast in 325° oven for 15 minutes. Remove excess grease from bottom of pan and baste duck with melted butter. Continue basting every 15 minutes during cooking time. A large duck will be cooked rare in approximately 30–40 minutes, medium in 45–60 minutes and well done in 1-1½ hours. A small duck, or teal, will be rare in approximately 20–30 minutes, medium in 30–40 minutes and well done in 45–50 minutes.

SHADOWS-ON-THE-TECHE SAUCE:

⅓ cup orange juice
¼ cup lemon juice
1 cup powdered sugar

2 tablespoons currant jelly
Grated rind of one lemon
1 tablespoon horse-radish

Combine ingredients and mix until smooth. Beat well. Heat and serve. The sauce may be made the preceeding day and kept in the refrigerator. Be sure to bring to room temperature before heating to serve.

TEAL ORLEANS

8 teals
1 stick butter
Salt
Pepper
1½ cups wine

¼ cup chopped parsley
2 tablespoons lemon juice
Garnish: water cress and thinly
    sliced lemon

Dry ducks, rub each cavity with 1 teaspoon butter and a generous amount of salt and pepper. Pour wine into baking dish; arrange ducks breast down, and bake in 450° oven for 10 minutes. Turn breasts up and continue baking

30–40 minutes, basting frequently. For well-done ducks, after turning breasts up, lower oven to 350° and cook, basting frequently, for 1½ hours. When ducks are cooked, place under broiler for 3 minutes to brown. Transfer 2 tablespoons pan juices to a saucepan; add remaining butter, parsley, lemon juice, and simmer for 3 minutes. Place teals on warm platter and spoon sauce over them. Garnish with water cress and lemon slices.

ROAST DOVE

16 slices bacon	2 tablespoons water
16 dove	16 slices French Bread (½" thick)
Salt	buttered and toasted
Pepper	Garnish: parsley sprigs
2 tablespoons butter	Giblet paste* (optional)

Boil bacon in water 10 minutes; remove and dry. Dry dove; salt and pepper generously inside and out. Wrap each dove with a slice of bacon. Warm a shallow baking pan; add 2 tablespoons butter to coat pan and arrange dove in a single layer, breast side down. Bake in 400° oven for 15 minutes. Turn breasts up and continue baking 15 minutes. Transfer pan juices to a saucepan adding 2 tablespoons water; simmer 2 minutes, skim grease and simmer an additional 2 minutes. Bacon may be removed if desired before browning doves under broiler for 3 minutes. Spread French bread with giblet paste and top with dove. Spoon sauce over breast, garnish with parsley and serve immediately.

* To make giblet paste, salt and pepper dove gizzards, hearts, and livers; sauté in small amount of butter for 1–2 minutes. Remove from pan and finely chop or grind giblets. Mash to a paste consistency adding a little more butter. Salt and pepper to taste.

VENISON GRILLADES

Salt	4 garlic cloves minced
Pepper	⅛ teaspoon thyme
8 shoulder steaks, 1½ inch thick	⅛ teaspoon sage
3 tablespoons flour	3 cups beef stock
4 tablespoons bacon grease	1⅓ cup sherry
2 cups minced green onions	⅛ teaspoon Tabasco
1 cup minced celery	½ cup minced parsley
½ cup minced green pepper	

Dry, salt, pepper, and dredge steaks in flour. On top of stove in a Dutch oven, brown steaks in bacon grease, remove; set aside. To bacon grease add green onions, celery, green pepper, garlic, thyme, and sage, cooking until onions are transparent, about 20 minutes. Replace steaks in pot, add stock, 1 cup sherry, and Tabasco. Cover and cook over low fire for 1½ to 2 hours. Before serving add ⅓ cup sherry and parsley simmering for 10 minutes. Serve with grits, spoon bread, or rice.

MEAT

All recipes are for eight portions unless otherwise stated.

DAUBE GLACÉ

2½ pounds boneless beef chuck
1½ pounds boneless pork
Salt
Pepper
3 tablespoons bacon grease
2 veal knuckles (broken in
   3 pieces)
3 onions, sliced
3 carrots, sliced
12 cloves, sliced
5 cloves garlic
8 sprigs parsley
5 bay leaves
1 teaspoon thyme
1 cup chopped celery
1 teaspoon allspice

½ teaspoon cayenne
3 cups beef bouillon
1 cup white wine
2 cups water
½ cup brandy
4 tablespoons gelatin
1 cup water
5 tablespoons lemon juice
3 tablespoons Worcestershire
2 tablespoons salt
½ teaspoon Tabasco
2 teaspoons white pepper
½ cup finely chopped pimento
Garnish: finely chopped parsley,
   lemon slices

Remove fat from meat; dry well. Salt and pepper meat. In a 6½-quart Dutch oven, sear meat in very hot bacon grease, browning well on all sides. Remove meat when browned and pour out bacon grease. Replace bones and seared meat in Dutch oven; add onions, carrots, cloves, garlic, parsley, bay leaf, thyme, celery, allspice, and cayenne. Pour in beef bouillon, wine, water, and brandy. Cover and simmer 3 hours. Remove meat, cool and dice. Strain stock through cheesecloth with several ice cubes to congeal grease. Soften gelatin in 1 cup water and heat to dissolve. To stock add lemon juice,

Worcestershire, salt, Tabasco, white pepper, pimento, and dissolved gelatin. Stir well. The stock should have a very salty and peppery taste as meat absorbs seasoning while jelling. Place diced meat in 2 oiled 1½-quart loaf-type Pyrex dishes. Slowly add seasoned stock. Chill. When jelled remove grease from top, unmold and slice with very sharp knife. Decorate with finely chopped parsley and lemon slices.

Alternate: To serve as hors d'oeuvres mold in a 3-quart rectangular Pyrex dish. Unmold; cut in small squares to fit on top of crackers.

GRILLADES

4 pounds beef/veal rounds,
    ½″ thick
½ cup bacon drippings
½ cup flour
1 cup chopped onions
2 cups chopped green onions
¾ cup chopped celery
1½ cups chopped green peppers
2 cloves garlic, minced
2 cups chopped tomatoes
½ teaspoon tarragon (optional)

⅔ teaspoon thyme
1 cup water
1 cup red wine
3 teaspoons salt
½ teaspoon black pepper
2 bay leaves
½ teaspoon Tabasco
2 tablespoons Worcestershire
    sauce
3 tablespoons chopped parsley

Remove fat from meat. Cut meat into serving-size pieces. Pound to ¼″ thick. In a Dutch oven brown meat well in 4 tablespoons bacon grease. As meat browns, remove to warm plate. To Dutch oven add 4 tablespoons bacon grease and flour. Stir and cook to make a dark brown roux. Add onions, green onions, celery, green pepper, garlic, and sauté until limp. Add tomatoes, tarragon, thyme, and cook for 3 minutes. Add water and wine. Stir well for several minutes; return meat; add salt, pepper, bay leaves, Tabasco, and Worcestershire. Lower heat, stir, and continue cooking. If veal rounds are used, simmer covered approximately 1 hour. If beef rounds are used, simmer covered approximately 2 hours. Remove bay leaves. Stir in parsley, cool, let the grillades sit several hours or overnight in refrigerator. More liquid may be added. Grillades should be very tender. Serve over grits or rice.

FILET DE BOEUF AUX CHAMPIGNONS

5–7 pounds tenderloin of beef
2 tablespoons olive oil
1 tablespoon salt
¼ teaspoon cayenne pepper
Freshly ground black pepper to
    taste

1 carrot, sliced
1 tablespoon chopped onion
4 tablespoons lemon juice
3 cups beef stock

Rub tenderloin with oil, salt, and pepper. Place in pan on top of carrot and onion; pour on lemon juice and let stand several hours. When ready to bake, pour the stock over the meat. Bake in 500° oven for 5 minutes, then turn oven to 350° and cook to desired doneness. Test with meat thermometer. Approximately 40 minutes for rare.

SAUCE:

3 tablespoons flour
6 tablespoons butter
2 cups stock from pan or beef
    stock

½ cup madeira
2 cups mushrooms
1½ dozen sliced truffles
    (optional)

Make a dark brown roux with flour and 2 tablespoons butter. Add stock and madeira; cook over medium heat 15 minutes. Sauté mushrooms and/or truffles in 4 tablespoons butter and add to the sauce. Serve warmed sauce in heated gravy boat.

SPICED BEEF

8 pounds sirloin tip roast
1½ ounces saltpeter (drugstore)
1½ cups salt
2 tablespoons coarsely ground
    pepper

1 ounce ground allspice
1 ounce ground cloves
½ ounce cinnamon
½ ounce nutmeg
2 cups dark molasses

Meat must be prepared 6 or 7 days prior to cooking.
   Mix salt, saltpeter, and pepper together. Rub meat well with half of this mixture. Place meat in crock and add remaining mixture to top of meat.

Mix spices and molasses together and pour over meat. Cover and place in refrigerator, 6 or 7 days, turning meat twice daily. When ready to cook, rinse meat in cold water. Place meat in large kettle. Cover meat completely with cold water and slowly bring to a boil. Cook 20 minutes per pound at a rolling boil. If serving as a main course, serve hot right after boiling, reserving water to store unused meat. Slice paper-thin for best results. If using as hors d'oeuvres or cold buffet, let meat cool in its water. When cool, place meat in its water in refrigerator until ready to serve. After serving, be sure to place remaining meat back in the water for storing.

STEAK AU POIVRE

8 steaks 1" thick (club, filet,
  or strip)
8 teaspoons cracked peppercorns
1 stick and 2 tablespoons butter
2 teaspoons oil
Salt
¼ cup finely chopped green onions

1 cup brown sauce (see index)
4 teaspoons lemon juice
4 teaspoons Worcestershire sauce
½ cup cognac
Garnish: ¼ cup chopped parsley
  or ¼ cup chopped chives
16 mushroom caps, sautéed

Trim all fat and gristle from steaks. Dry well. Rub and press approximately ½ teaspoon cracked peppercorns into each side of steaks; let sit for 1 hour. Use two large frying pans; place 1 tablespoon butter and 1 teaspoon oil in each. Over very high heat, let butter brown before searing steaks on both sides. Cook to desired doneness, approximately 1 minute each side for rare steaks. Transfer steaks to warm platter; sprinkle lightly with salt and keep warm. Drain grease from pans and scrape residue of one pan into the other pan. To the residue add 4 tablespoons butter; sauté green onions several minutes, add brown sauce, lemon juice, and Worcestershire sauce. Stir and cook over low heat 1 minute. Remove from heat and swish 4 tablespoons butter into sauce until melted. Spoon sauce over steaks. Warm cognac, ignite, and pour over steaks. Garnish with chopped parsley or chives and sautéed mushroom caps.

VEAL BIRDS

20 veal cutlets, pounded to 3 x 5"
Salt
Pepper

Thyme
Bacon grease
1 cup dry white wine

Salt and pepper cutlets and dust lightly with thyme. Quickly brown cutlets in a small amount of bacon grease, a few at a time, and set aside. Pour off excess grease, add wine to the scrapings, stir, and reserve this liquid.

STUFFING:

½ pound pork sausage, sliced
½ pound bacon
1 cup chopped onions
½ cup chopped green onions
¼ cup minced parsley
Salt
Pepper
Worcestershire sauce

Tabasco
1½ cups toasted and crumbled
   French bread
20 wooden toothpicks
1½ cups mushrooms
½ stick butter
Bouillon if necessary

In a large skillet cook sausage; drain, reserving drippings, and set aside. Fry bacon; remove, crumble, and set aside. In bacon drippings slowly cook onions and green onions until transparent; add parsley, sausage, bacon, salt, pepper, Worcestershire, Tabasco, and bread crumbs. Mix well. Sausage drippings may be added if mixture is too dry. Make birds by adding some stuffing to individual cutlets; roll each, secure with toothpicks, and place in large shallow baking dish. Sauté mushrooms in butter. Pour the wine liquid over birds, add mushrooms, cover and bake in 350° oven about 45 minutes. If liquid is not ¼" deep in bottom of baking dish, add bouillon or additional wine. Remove toothpicks before serving.

VEAL AND HAM WITH ARTICHOKES

4 pounds boneless veal cut in
   1" cubes
Salt
Pepper
7 tablespoons cooking oil
1 cup chopped onions
⅓ cup chopped celery
1 clove garlic, minced

4 tablespoons flour
1 quart water
2 cups diced ham
½ pound fresh mushrooms, sliced
½ cup marsala wine
¼ cup chopped parsley
8 boiled artichokes

Season veal with salt and pepper and let it stand about one hour. In a 4-quart Dutch oven, brown veal in 3 tablespoons cooking oil or oil that just covers the bottom of the pot. Remove veal, and sauté onions, celery, and garlic until limp. In separate pan make a dark brown roux with flour and 4 tablespoons cooking oil. Put veal back into pot with seasoning; add water and bring all to a boil. Slowly add the roux, stirring constantly. Cover, leaving tiny crack for steam to escape, and simmer 30 minutes. Then add ham, mushrooms, and marsala; simmer an additional 45 minutes. Let sit for several hours or refrigerate overnight. When ready to reheat, salt and pepper to taste, add parsley, and serve over warmed artichoke bottoms, using artichoke leaves to decorate around the plate and for dipping into the gravy.

Alternate: When ready to reheat, salt and pepper to taste, add parsley and chopped artichoke bottoms, and serve over rice.

VEAL POCKET

1 large veal pocket	*2 cups sliced mushrooms*
Salt	*1 cup minced ham*
Pepper	*2 cups fresh bread crumbs*
5 tablespoons olive oil	*1 cup milk*
8 tablespoons finely chopped	*Sprinkle of marjoram*
onions	*Sprinkle of thyme*
2 cloves garlic, minced	*1 tablespoon flour*
¼ teaspoon Tabasco	*Garnish: lemon slices*

GRAVY:

½ cup finely chopped celery	*2 bay leaves*
½ cup finely chopped green pepper	*2 cups beef stock*
½ cup finely chopped white onions	*1 cup white or rosé wine*

Salt and pepper veal pocket inside and out; rub outside with 1 tablespoon olive oil. In remaining oil sauté onions, garlic, and Tabasco until soft, but not brown. Add mushrooms and ham and cook 5 minutes. Remove from heat; add bread crumbs and milk, mix. Place stuffing in pocket and either sew or close with small skewers and tie firmly. Lightly rub outside of meat with marjoram and thyme. Sift flour on top.

    Prepare gravy by adding celery, green pepper, onions, and bay leaves to beef stock. Place meat on rack in roasting pan and bake in 500° oven for 25–30 minutes until brown. Reduce heat to 375°; add gravy and cook an additional 20 minutes per pound. Meat should be basted occasionally. Veal should be well done, but not dry. After removing meat, thicken gravy with just a bit of flour dissolved in hot water, and cook a few minutes longer on top of stove. Remove excess grease and bay leaves. Add wine. Garnish veal pocket with lemon slices and serve gravy in a warmed sauceboat. Slice meat thin.

VEAL LORRAINE

16 veal rib chops
1 cup diced, lean raw bacon
2 tablespoons butter
Salt
Pepper
4 green onions, finely chopped

2 teaspoons chopped parsley
1 cup sliced mushrooms
1 cup stock
1 cup dry white wine
4 egg yolks, beaten
2 teaspoons lemon juice

Remove bones and fat from chops. Dry and set aside. In heavy skillet, sauté bacon in butter. Add chops and sprinkle with salt and pepper. Cook about 20 minutes, over low fire, turning from time to time. Remove bacon and chops with slotted spoon and keep warm. Pour off most of fat. Add green onions, parsley, and mushrooms. Stir mixture for a minute, but do not brown. Add stock and wine, stirring in all the good brown juices sticking to the pan. Add pinch of salt and a little pepper; cook until the liquid is reduced a little. Remove from fire and add a little of the hot liquid to the beaten egg yolks before adding egg yolks to skillet. Heat the sauce over a very low flame, stirring constantly, but do not let boil. Return the chops and bacon to the sauce and add lemon juice. If prepared ahead of time, be sure to reheat in double boiler, to prevent curdling.

STUFFED HAM

10–12 pound ham, deboned
1 cup ham (from cavity) finely
  ground
3 cups Ritz crackers, finely
  crumbled
1½ tablespoons dry mustard
2 tablespoons dark brown sugar
½ cup finely chopped celery
1 cup finely chopped onions
1 cup finely chopped mushrooms

1 finely chopped green pepper
½ stick butter
1 teaspoon sage
1 tablespoon vinegar
½ cup chopped parsley
2 eggs beaten
¼ cup madeira
Garnish: pineapple rings and
  cherries

GLAZE:

¼ cup madeira
1 cup prepared mustard

⅓ cup dark brown sugar

Enlarge bone cavity removing enough ham to form a 3″ pocket. Trim excess fat from ham and make crosswise slashes on top. Mix ground ham, crackers, dry mustard, and 2 tablespoons dark brown sugar together. Sauté celery, onions, mushrooms, and green pepper in butter until no liquid remains. Add to dry mixture. Mix in sage, vinegar, parsley, eggs, and ¼ cup madeira. Stuff ham and secure with skewers if necessary. Arrange pineapple rings and cherries on top and secure with toothpicks. Prepare glaze by combining ¼ cup madeira, prepared mustard, and ⅓ cup brown sugar; smooth over top of ham. Bake in 350° oven for 45 minutes, basting frequently with glaze. Chill 24 hours; remove toothpicks and slice thin.

PORK WITH ORANGE SAUCE

5-pound loin of pork (have butcher crack bones) or
8 pork chops 1″ thick

MARINADE:

½ cup lemon juice
½ cup soy sauce
½ cup marsala (or red) wine

½ teaspoon pressed garlic
2 teaspoons ground ginger

In a shallow dish combine marinade ingredients and pour over pork. Refrigerate, covered, overnight, turning occasionally. Remove pork; reserve marinade for basting. Cook loin on spit or chops on barbecue pit about eight inches from coals. If meat thermometer is used in loin, temperature should reach 185° (about 2 hours). Baste often. If preferred, cook in 350° oven, basting often, approximately 2½ hours (185° on thermometer). Pork chops should be browned and fully cooked. Pour orange sauce over loin or chops.

ORANGE SAUCE:

⅔ cup granulated sugar
1 tablespoon cornstarch
½ teaspoon salt
20 whole cloves, tied in a
   cheesecloth bag

½ teaspoon cinnamon
1 tablespoon grated orange rind
1 cup orange juice
8 orange slices, halved

Place sugar, cornstarch, salt, cloves, cinnamon, orange rind, and orange juice in a saucepan and cook over medium heat until thickened and clear. Remove cloves, add orange slices, cover, and remove from heat.

STUFFED PORK CHOPS

1 stick butter
½ cup chopped onions
1 cup chopped green onions
½ cup chopped celery
¼ cup chopped green pepper
2 garlic cloves, crushed
1½ cups herb stuffing
3 tablespoons chopped parsley
1 cup chicken stock

1 egg beaten
9 (1½") pork chops with pocket
   cut in side, fat trimmed
Salt
Pepper
Hot fat, or fat cut off chops
Milk or cream
8 lemon slices
¼ cup chopped parsley (garnish)

(Needed: heavy needle and thread)

In a skillet, melt butter and sauté onions, green onions, celery, green pepper, and garlic until soft but not brown. Add herb stuffing and 3 tablespoons parsley. Toss. Add enough stock to moisten dressing so it will hold together; add egg and mix. Fill each pork chop pocket with about 1 tablespoon of stuffing and sew together. (You may skewer, but it is then difficult to sear them.) Salt and pepper chops and brown them in fat from pork chops or hot fat. When browned remove and arrange, in a single layer, in flat greased casserole dish. Pour a little cream or milk to barely cover bottom of dish and bake in 350° oven for 1 hour. Garnish with lemon slices and parsley.

RED BEANS AND RICE

1 ham bone
11½ cups water
2 teaspoons garlic salt
¼ teaspoon Tabasco
1 teaspoon Worcestershire sauce
1 pound red beans, washed
1 cup chopped celery
1 cup chopped onions
1½ cloves garlic, minced

3 tablespoons oil
½ pound ham, cubed
¼ pound hot sausage, sliced
½ pound smoked sausage, sliced
2 bay leaves
Salt to taste
Pepper to taste, coarse ground
¼ cup chopped parsley
2 cups cooked rice

In a large pot or Dutch oven place ham bone, water, garlic salt, Tabasco, Worcestershire, and beans. Cook, uncovered, over low flame. Sauté celery, onions, and garlic in oil until transparent. In another pan sauté ham and sausage; drain. Add cooked meats and seasoning to beans. Add bay leaves, salt, and pepper and continue to cook over low flame until beans are soft and creamy. Approximately 2½ hours. Remove bay leaves and add parsley before serving. For additional thickness cook longer. Serve over hot, fluffy rice.

LAMB WITH FRUIT DRESSING

Crown round of lamb†
Olive oil

Salt
Pepper

GLAZE:

½ cup orange marmalade
1 tablespoon brown sugar
2 teaspoons prepared mustard

3 tablespoons lemon juice
Garnish: orange slices and
*   maraschino cherries*

† Rack (20–24 ribs) or leg of lamb may be substituted for crown round.

Rub lamb with oil, salt, and pepper. Place foil on bone ends. Place in roasting pan and bake in 325° oven for 1 hour and 25 minutes, or until meat thermometer registers 175° to 180°, or to your desired doneness. In a saucepan blend marmalade, brown sugar, mustard, lemon juice; heat. During last 30 minutes of cooking time, baste lamb with hot glaze.

FRUIT DRESSING:

1½ cups white raisins
Sherry to cover
2 cups diced peeled apples
1 cup finely chopped onions
2 garlic cloves, minced
2 sticks butter
2 tablespoons lemon juice

⅛ teaspoon each; mace, nutmeg
* thyme, rosemary and chervil*
3 tablespoons minced parsley
2 cups toasted seasoned bread
* crumbs*
2 tablespoons roasting juices

While roast is cooking, prepare dressing. Plump raisins in warm sherry to cover. Sauté apples, onions, and garlic in butter until soft. Add plumped raisins, sherry, lemon juice, herbs, and parsley. Cook over low flame for 15 minutes, then add bread crumbs and roasting juices. Toss to mix well and heat to serve. When roast is done, place hot dressing in a bowl and place in the center of the crown round, or in a side dish for the leg of lamb. Remove the foil; garnish with orange slices and cherries.

CURRY SAUCE FOR MEATS, CHICKEN, OR SEAFOOD

1 onion, sliced
1 carrot, sliced
1 celery stalk, sliced
3 tablespoons butter
3 to 4 tablespoons curry powder
½ teaspoon chili powder
3 tablespoons flour
2 cups coconut milk*
Salt to taste
⅛ teaspoon mace

⅛ teaspoon allspice
⅛ teaspoon nutmeg
⅛ teaspoon ground cloves
⅛ teaspoon cinnamon
1 apple, chopped
2 tablespoons currant jelly
2 tablespoons chopped chutney
5 cups cooked lamb or chicken cut
* in bite-size pieces or*
5 cups cleaned, boiled shrimp

* To make coconut milk, use one coconut per cup of regular milk. Boil milk and put in blender with coconut meat and the liquid from the coconut. Puree and strain through cheese cloth.

Cook onion, carrot, and celery in butter until soft. Add curry and chili powder, and cook for 5 minutes. Blend in flour. Add coconut milk, and stir until just boiling. Add salt, mace, allspice, nutmeg, cloves, cinnamon, and apple. Simmer ½ hour and put through strainer. This much should be made a day ahead and allowed to set overnight. Put sauce in double boiler, heat, and add meat, chicken, or seafood. Add currant jelly and chutney. If mixture is too thick after heating, thin with meat or seafood stock. Serve with rice and side dishes of chopped eggs, bacon, green peppers, peanuts, pimentos, mashed bananas, pumpkin seeds, etc. Freezes well.

SALADS, SALAD DRESSINGS, SAUCES, PRESERVES

All recipes are for eight portions unless otherwise stated.

AVOCADO AND GRAPEFRUIT SALAD

Sections from 3 or 4 fresh grapefruit
3 avocados, sliced
Lettuce

DRESSING:

2 cups salad oil
1 cup cider vinegar
½ cup ketchup
2 tablespoons salt

6 tablespoons sugar
1 small onion, grated
Dash of pepper

In a blender combine oil, vinegar, ketchup, salt, sugar, onion, and pepper; set at high speed and blend thoroughly. Makes about 1 quart.

CHICKEN SALAD AND DRESSING

1 large baking hen (about
6½ pounds)
2 teaspoons salt
½ teaspoon pepper
3 celery tops
2 carrots, sliced
2 bay leaves
1 large onion, quartered

5 sprigs parsley
1 clove garlic
1 lemon, quartered and squeezed
1 apple, peeled and diced
⅔ cup chopped celery
1 2½-ounce bottle capers, drained
Boiled dressing

Cover hen with water; add salt, pepper, celery tops, carrots, bay leaves, onion, parsley, garlic, lemon juice, and quartered lemon. Boil for 2½ hours. Remove hen and let cool. Skin and cut chicken into bite size pieces; mix with apple, celery, and capers. Add only enough chilled boiled dressing to bind together. Serve on lettuce with mayonnaise.

BOILED DRESSING:

3 egg yolks
6 tablespoons corn or salad oil
1 cup milk or chicken stock or
    ½ cup milk and ½ cup stock
1 teaspoon sugar

1 tablespoon flour
1½ tablespoons dry mustard
1½ teaspoons salt
¼ cup cider vinegar, heated

In top of double boiler, not over heat, beat egg yolks until pale yellow. Add oil very slowly, beating constantly. Add all other ingredients except vinegar. Stir and put over heat being sure water does not touch bottom of double boiler. Cook and stir until dressing coats a silver spoon; then add hot vinegar and cook a few minutes, stirring constantly. Chill. Good with chicken salad, deviled eggs, or cole slaw.

COLE SLAW

SLAW:

2 medium-size onions, thinly
    sliced
2 heads cabbage, shredded

1 green pepper, thinly sliced
2 ounces capers, drained
    (optional)

Soak onions in ice water for several hours before serving. Drain well. Toss cabbage, onions, and peppers together.

DRESSING:

3 cups mayonnaise
1 tablespoon celery seed
1 tablespoon dill seed
2 tablespoons prepared mustard

6 tablespoons lemon or lime juice
3 tablespoons sugar
Salt to taste
Freshly ground black pepper

Combine mayonnaise, celery seed, dill seed, mustard, citrus juice, and sugar. Mix well. Pour dressing on slaw. Salt and pepper to taste. Add capers, if desired. Serve cold.

SHRIMP RING

2 tablespoons gelatin
1 cup consommé
8 ounces cream cheese
¾ cup mayonnaise
2 cups chopped, boiled shrimp*
1 cup chopped celery
2 pimentos, chopped
1 bottle capers, drained

2 tablespoons grated onions
½ cup chili sauce
2 tablespoons lemon juice
2 teaspoons Worcestershire sauce
¼ cup chopped parsley
1 teaspoon salt
¼ teaspoon pepper
2 drops Tabasco

Soften gelatin in ¼ cup consommé. Heat remaining consommé; add softened gelatin to dissolve. Cool. In a bowl beat cream cheese and mayonnaise with a wooden spoon until well blended. Add cooled consommé and all other ingredients. Place in a lightly greased 2-quart ring mold or fish mold. Chill. Serve on lettuce with French dressing. Can be prepared the day before serving.

* Boiled crawfish tails may be substituted.

SPINACH SALAD

DRESSING:

1 cup oil (not olive)
5 tablespoons red wine vinegar
4 tablespoons sour cream
1½ teaspoons salt
½ teaspoon dry mustard

2 tablespoons sugar
Coarsely ground black pepper
2 teaspoons chopped parsley
2 cloves garlic, crushed

SALAD:

2 10-ounce packages fresh spinach, washed and dried
4 hard-boiled eggs, chopped
8 strips bacon, crisply fried and crumbled

Mix dressing at least 6 hours before using. Toss spinach with desired amount of dressing before serving. Top with eggs and bacon.

FRENCH DRESSING

¾ cup olive oil
¼ cup wine vinegar
¼ teaspoon Worcestershire sauce
1 clove garlic, cut in half
1 teaspoon sugar

½ teaspoon salt
¼ teaspoon paprika
¼ teaspoon dry mustard
⅛ teaspoon pepper
⅛ teaspoon thyme

Combine all ingredients and refrigerate. Remove garlic, shake well before serving.

POPPY SEED DRESSING

1 cup sugar
2 teaspoons dry mustard
1 teaspoon salt
⅔ cup cider vinegar

2 teaspoons onion juice
2 cups salad oil
1 tablespoon poppy seeds

Combine sugar, mustard, salt, vinegar, and onion juice, mixing well. Add oil gradually and then add poppy seeds. Serve over fresh fruit of the season. Yield 3 cups. Keep refrigerated.

ROQUEFORT DRESSING

¼ pound Roquefort or blue cheese
½ cup homemade mayonnaise
½ cup light cream
½ cup sour cream
2 tablespoons lemon juice
1 teaspoon grated onion

2 tablespoons chopped parsley
1 teaspoon Worcestershire sauce
¼ teaspoon garlic salt
¼ teaspoon black pepper
1 teaspoon salt

Mash cheese in a mixing bowl. Add all other ingredients and mix well. Yields 2 cups. Keep refrigerated.

VINAIGRETTE DRESSING

1 tablespoon water
2 whole eggs
1 teaspoon dry mustard
1 or 2 garlic cloves
1 teaspoon pepper

1 teaspoon paprika
1 teaspoon salt
1 cup wine vinegar
3 cups olive oil or salad oil

In a bowl, using a wire whisk, combine water, eggs, mustard, garlic, pepper, paprika, and salt. Boil vinegar and slowly blend with first mixture. Gradually blend in oil. Refrigerate.

BÉARNAISE SAUCE

3 sticks lightly salted butter
½ cup tarragon wine vinegar
½ cup dry vermouth
2 tablespoons finely minced green
  onions
2 tablespoons finely minced
  parsley
1 teaspoon dried tarragon or
  1 tablespoon minced fresh
  tarragon
2 teaspoons dried chervil

10 cracked peppercorns
7 egg yolks
3 teaspoons warm water
½ teaspoon salt
Black pepper to taste
2 tablespoons chopped chives
  (optional)
2 tablespoons chopped parsley
  (optional)
6 thin slices butter, room
  temperature

In a saucepan melt butter, clarify, and set aside. In separate saucepan combine vinegar, vermouth, green onions, parsley, tarragon, chervil, and peppercorns. Over high heat reduce this liquid until it barely covers bottom of pan. Cool mixture by setting this pan in cold water before adding to eggs. In a heavy saucepan, not over heat, place egg yolks, water, and cooled reduced vinegar mixture, beating with a wire whisk until frothy, approximately 3–5 minutes. Place over low heat, and continue beating vigorously several minutes longer. Pan should be removed from heat often during this process to ensure slow cooking. Beat constantly until it is the consistency of a thick cream sauce.

Remove from fire, continue beating, and slowly add clarified butter to mixture, a tablespoon at a time, until all butter is used. Add salt, parsley or chives, while beating in well. If mixture curdles, add 1 tablespoon cold water and beat vigorously. To prevent scum from forming on top, cover sauce with 6 thin slices of butter and place on top of stove near pilot light or place in double boiler over lukewarm water. You may add a tablespoon of warm water and beat again before serving. Yields 2 cups.

BARBECUE SAUCE

1 stick butter
1 cup water
1 cup vinegar
1 cup ketchup
2 tablespoons lemon juice
½ cup Worcestershire sauce
1 teaspoon sugar

1 tablespoon chili powder
1 tablespoon dry mustard
1 cup minced onions
1 large clove garlic, minced
Red pepper to taste
Salt to taste

Combine all ingredients and bring to a boil. Reduce heat and simmer at least 1 hour. Baste chicken or pork ribs. Refrigerates or freezes well. Yields approximately 4 cups.

BROWN SAUCE

¾ cup coarsely chopped onions
¾ cup coarsely chopped carrot
6 tablespoons butter
6 tablespoons flour
3½ cups beef stock or bouillon
1½ cups dry white wine
2 ribs celery

3 sprigs parsley
1 small bay leaf
2 cloves garlic
½ teaspoon thyme
¼ teaspoon black pepper, freshly
    ground
1 tablespoon tomato paste

In a 4½-quart heavy pot sauté onions and carrot in butter on high flame for about 10 minutes or until onion is browned. Slowly add flour and continue stirring, cooking until dark brown. Be careful not to burn! Add stock, wine, celery, parsley, bay leaf, garlic, thyme, and pepper. Simmer sauce, uncovered, about 1 hour, stirring occasionally until sauce is reduced to half the amount. Add tomato paste; stir. Remove from fire. Strain. Do not press ingredients through sieve. Yield 2–2½ cups. Sauce may be frozen.

CREOLE SAUCE

¼ cup flour
¼ cup bacon grease
2 cups chopped onions
½ cup chopped green onions
2 cloves garlic, minced
1 cup chopped green pepper
1 cup chopped celery and some
  leaves
1 teaspoon thyme
2 bay leaves

3 teaspoons salt
½ teaspoon pepper
6 ounces tomato paste
1 16-ounce can tomatoes and
  liquid
8 ounces tomato sauce
1 teaspoon Tabasco
½ cup chopped parsley
1 tablespoon lemon juice

In a large skillet or Dutch oven, make a dark brown roux of flour and bacon grease. Add onions, green onions, green pepper, garlic, celery and leaves, thyme, bay leaves, salt, and pepper; sauté, uncovered, over medium flame until onions are transparent and soft, about 30 minutes. Add tomato paste; sauté 3 additional minutes. Add diced tomatoes with liquid and tomato sauce; simmer very slowly, partially covered, for 1 hour, stirring occasionally. Add Tabasco, parsley, and lemon juice; stir, cover, and remove from heat. Best to let set several hours or overnight. Makes about 4 cups. Remove bay leaf before serving. Freezes well.

HOLLANDAISE SAUCE

3 sticks lightly salted butter
7 egg yolks
2 teaspoons warm water
2 tablespoons lemon juice
½ teaspoon salt
¼ teaspoon white pepper

⅛ teaspoon cayenne (optional)
2 tablespoons chopped parsley
  (optional)
6 thin slices butter, room
  temperature

In a saucepan melt butter, clarify, and set aside. In a heavy saucepan, not over heat, place egg yolks, water, and lemon juice; beat together vigorously with wire whisk until frothy, approximately 3–5 minutes. Place over low heat and continue beating vigorously several minutes longer. Pan should be removed from heat often during this process to ensure slow cooking. Beat constantly until mixture is the consistency of a thick cream sauce.

Remove from fire, continue beating, and slowly add clarified butter, a tablespoon at a time, until all butter is used. Add salt, pepper, cayenne, and parsley, beating in well. If mixture curdles, add 1 tablespoon cold water and beat vigorously. To prevent scum from forming on top, cover sauce with thin slices of butter and place on top of stove near pilot light or place in double boiler over lukewarm water. May add a tablespoon of warm water and beat again before serving. Yields 2 cups.

FISH SAUCE

2 cups mayonnaise (see index)
4 hard-boiled eggs, mashed with
    fork
6 small green onions, finely
    chopped

2½-ounce jar capers, drained
1½ teaspoons dry mustard
5 tablespoons lemon juice
1 teaspoon Worcestershire sauce
7 drops Tabasco

Combine above ingredients and refrigerate at least 1 hour before serving. Makes 4 cups. Serve with cold red snapper, crabmeat, or any fried seafood.

HOT MUSTARD

3 egg yolks
1 cup sugar
1 cup vinegar

1 teaspoon salt
2 ounces dry mustard

Blend all ingredients together until smooth. Cook in double boiler 30 minutes until very thick. Chill.

HOT PEPPER SAUCE

Hot green or red peppers   Vinegar*

Fill a cruet with washed peppers. Heat vinegar and pour in cruet, enough to cover peppers. Replace cruet cover and let stand several weeks. Use on red beans and rice, black-eyed peas, greens, or cabbage.

* Sherry may be used instead of vinegar, but do not heat sherry. Use sherry pepper sauce in turtle soup.

MARCHAND de VIN

6 ounces mushrooms sliced
6 tablespoons butter
1 cup minced green onions
1½ cups dry red wine
1½ cups brown sauce (see index)

1 tablespoon lemon juice
¼ teaspoon black pepper
½ teaspoon salt
1 tablespoon cognac (optional)

In a small skillet sauté mushrooms in 2 tablespoons butter and set aside. Melt 4 tablespoons butter, and sauté onions over medium heat for 10 minutes, until wilted. Add wine, and cook down until sauce is brown and liquid is almost evaporated. Stir in brown sauce, cook several minutes before adding mushrooms, lemon juice, pepper, and salt. Before serving stir in 1 tablespoon cognac, if desired, and cook 1 minute. Makes about 1⅔ cups. Can be frozen.

CHOW CHOW

2 heads cauliflower
2 small cabbages
3 green tomatoes
3 cucumbers
6 green peppers
6 onions
6 pods hot peppers
Water to cover
1 cup salt
5 cups cider vinegar

1 teaspoon powdered cloves
1 tablespoon ground allspice
1 tablespoon celery seed
¼ cup flour
¼ cup sugar
1 tablespoon cayenne
4 ounces dry mustard
1 tablespoon turmeric
1 cup olive oil

Use a combination of vegetables that equals 12 pounds. Cut vegetables very fine or leave in pieces, as desired. Cover with water and 1 cup salt. Let stand overnight. Next day, drain vegetables well and place in large pot. Add 4 cups vinegar, cloves, allspice, celery seed; bring to a hard boil and remove from fire. Make a paste with flour, sugar, cayenne, mustard, turmeric, 1 cup vinegar, and olive oil. Mix well and cook until thick, about three minutes. Slowly stir paste into vegetables, bring to a boil, remove from heat, and seal in hot, sterilized jars. Makes 12 pints.

MAYONNAISE

2 tablespoons lemon juice
1 teaspoon salt
1½ teaspoons prepared mustard
1 teaspoon sugar
2 egg yolks

1 pint chilled salad oil
Optional:
  12 drops Tabasco
  3 tablespoons capers

Place lemon juice, salt, mustard, and sugar in an electric mixer and mix on medium high speed until blended. Add egg yolks, one at a time. Add oil gradually by droplets until mayonnaise thickens, then add oil faster. Makes about 2½ cups.

CHUTNEY

6 pounds mangoes, peeled
4 pounds peeled apples or pears,
  or combine, as desired
1 quart cider vinegar
5 pounds white sugar
15 ounces rasins
10 garlic cloves, pressed
1½ cups finely chopped green
  pepper
2 limes, juice and grated rind

1 large onion, finely chopped
⅓ cup candied ginger, cut in
  strips
2 tablespoons salt
1 teaspoon cinnamon
1 teaspoon ground cloves
1 teaspoon allspice
1 tablespoon mustard seed
½ teaspoon cayenne pepper

Cut fruit into small pieces or slices. Put vinegar and sugar into a large pot, bring to a boil, add fruit and other ingredients. Simmer approximately 2 hours, or until fruit is tender and sauce thick. Stir carefully to prevent sticking. Pour chutney into hot, sterilized jars and seal. Wait 2 weeks to open. Delicious with meat, shrimp Creole, or over cream cheese as an hors d'oeuvre. Makes 8 to 10 pints.

FIG PRESERVES

6 pounds ripe figs, stems removed
¾ cup soda
Water to cover figs

6 pounds sugar
16 lemon slices
8 cinnamon sticks

Using large enamel bowl or crock, soak figs in soda water for 1 hour. Drain and rinse well. Place figs in large shallow roasting pan and sprinkle sugar over all. Pour in 2 to 3 cups water, enough so the bottom of the pan is covered. Add lemon slices and cinnamon sticks. Bring to a vigorous boil, turn down fire so that there is always bubbling on top. Do not stir very often. Cook 1½–2 hours or until figs are easily pierced with a straw. Some figs will split, but whole figs are desired. Take off scum. Fill sterilized jars, being sure 2 slices of lemon and one cinnamon stick are in each. Makes 8 pints. Fig preserves are delicious on biscuits or toast. For a special treat, warm and serve over vanilla ice cream.

PICKLED FIGS

½ cup baking soda
Water
1 gallon fresh figs, stems
  removed
8 cups sugar

3 cups cider vinegar
2 tablespoons each, pickling
  spice and whole allspice,
  secured in a cheesecloth bag
3 fresh cinnamon sticks

Dissolve soda in 2½ cups water or water to cover figs. Add figs and let soak 5 minutes. Drain and rinse several times. In a large, shallow pan (small roasting pan) combine 5 cups water, sugar, vinegar, bagged spices, and cinnamon. Bring to a vigorous boil; add figs and return to a gentle boil for 10 minutes or until they turn clear. Take off heat, remove scum, and let figs stand in solution for 24 hours. Heat to a simmer. Be sure figs are thoroughly heated. Take out spice bag and cinnamon sticks. Seal in sterilized jars. Wait several weeks before opening. Makes 6 pints.

PEPPER JELLY

1 cup minced green pepper
½ cup minced hot pepper or
  2–4 tablespoons Tabasco

1½ cups cider vinegar
6½ cups sugar
1 bottle Certo

In blender, place green pepper, hot pepper or Tabasco, and cider vinegar; blend for a few seconds. In a 6-quart saucepan, combine pepper mixture and sugar; rapidly bring to a rolling boil that cannot be stirred down. Remove from heat for 10 minutes; skim off froth. Stir in Certo and seal in hot, sterilized jars. Makes 6 or 7 half pints.

SWEETS AND PARTY BREADS

All recipes are for eight portions unless otherwise stated.

ALMOND TART

1 stick butter, softened
1 cup light brown sugar, sifted
1 egg
1 cup sliced almonds, toasted and
   ground in blender for 5 seconds
¼ teaspoon almond extract

1 cup whipping cream
Additional ¾ cup sliced almonds,
   toasted and ground in blender
   for 5 seconds, for decoration
   (optional)

Beat butter until light and fluffy; gradually add sugar, beating well after each addition. Add egg, beating for a minute. Fold in 1 cup almonds and almond extract. Mix well. Place on foil and refrigerate for 1 hour. Shape a log approximately 8 inches long and 2 inches in diameter. If desired, cover log with additional almonds. Carefully wrap in aluminum foil and place in freezer. To serve, let stand at room temperature for 10 minutes, cut into 1" slices, and frost with whipped cream. Keeps in freezer up to 3 months.

BASIC PIE CRUST

1¼ cups flour
¼ teaspoon salt
Pinch of sugar

1 stick butter (chilled)
¼ cup vegetable shortening
3 to 4 tablespoons ice water

Sift flour, salt, and sugar into large mixing bowl. Cut butter and shortening into small pieces and cut into flour mixture rapidly. When shortening is the size of tiny peas, add water gradually, mixing lightly until dough holds together. Don't overwork. Shape into a ball and refrigerate for ½ hour. Place on a floured surface and roll out to ⅛" thickness, 2" larger than pie pan. Transfer to pan by rolling dough onto rolling pin and unroll into pan. Trim edges and flute. Dough can be refrigerated several days before using or it can be frozen. Prick bottom of shell to bake. Cook in 400° oven until golden brown. Approximately 10 minutes. Yields one 10" pie crust.

BREAD PUDDING WITH COGNAC SAUCE

2 cups milk
½ stick butter
½ cup sugar
4 cups French bread cubes, a day old
½ cup raisins

2 eggs, beaten
⅛ teaspoon salt
½ teaspoon nutmeg
1 teaspoon vanilla
¼ cup shredded coconut (optional)

Scald milk. Melt butter in milk, and stir in sugar. Pour over bread and raisins. Let stand 15 minutes. Add beaten eggs, salt, nutmeg, vanilla, and coconut. Bake in a well-greased 1½-quart dish at 350° for 35 to 45 minutes. Serve warm, topped with cognac sauce.

COGNAC SAUCE:

1 stick butter
2 cups confectioners' sugar
¼ cup cognac

Cream butter and sugar and gradually add cognac.

BROWNIES WITH CARAMEL ICING

1 cup white sugar
1 stick butter, softened
2 eggs, separated
4 tablespoons cocoa

½ cup flour
1 cup chopped pecans
1 teaspoon vanilla

Cream sugar and butter. Add egg yolks, cocoa, flour, pecans, and vanilla. Fold in stiffly beaten egg whites. Put into a greased 8 x 8" pan. Bake in 350° oven for 30–35 minutes.

CARAMEL ICING:

1 pound brown sugar

1 cup whipping cream

1 stick butter

1 teaspoon vanilla

Boil sugar, cream, and butter to soft-ball stage. Remove from fire and add vanilla. Beat until thick and cool enough to spread. This makes enough icing for two recipes of brownies. Also delicious on cake.

CARAMEL SQUARES

1 stick butter, softened

1 pound light brown sugar

1 cup flour

1 teaspoon baking powder

1 teaspoon salt

1½ teaspoons vanilla

4 eggs

1½ cups chopped pecans

Garnish: 1 pint whipping cream
    (optional)

Cream butter and sugar. Add flour, baking powder, salt, and vanilla. Mix. Add eggs and pecans. Mix. Pour into a greased flat pan 13 x 9 x 2" and bake in 375° oven for 20–30 minutes. Cool, then cut into squares, or cut into eight portions and top with whipped cream.

CHEESE CAKE

CRUST:

6 ounces Zwieback

½ stick butter, room temperature

2 tablespoons sugar

FILLING:

24 ounces cream cheese at room temperature

1 cup sugar

5 eggs

TOPPING:

> *1 pint sour cream*
> *¾ cup sugar*
> *1 teaspoon vanilla*

Roll Zwieback into fine crumbs. Add soft butter and sugar, mixing well. Spread on bottom and sides of an 8″ spring-form pan and set aside. Cream the cheese, add sugar, and mix well. Add whole eggs, one at a time, mixing well after each addition. Pour mixture into pan. Bake in 350° oven for 45 minutes. Remove from oven; let stand for ½ hour. Mix sour cream, sugar, and vanilla. Pour on top of baked cake. Return to 450° oven for 10 minutes. Refrigerate when cool. You may reserve about 2 or 3 tablespoons of the crumb mixture to sprinkle on top of the sour cream mixture before returning to the oven.

CHOCOLATE ROLL WITH CHOCOLATE SAUCE

> *5 eggs, separated*
> *½ cup sugar*
> *1 tablespoon flour*
> *2 tablespoons cocoa*
> *⅛ teaspoon salt*
> *¼ teaspoon cream of tartar*

> *1 cup whipping cream*
> *2 tablespoons powdered sugar*
> *1 teaspoon vanilla or 1 teaspoon*
>   *cognac*
> *Tiny pinch of salt*

Beat egg yolks and sugar together until the mixture forms a ribbon. Add flour and cocoa and mix well. Beat egg whites, adding salt and cream of tartar as they thicken, continuing to beat until very stiff. Fold whites into chocolate mixture until whites no longer show. Pour batter into 15½ x 10½ x 1″ pan which has been well greased and lined with greased wax paper. Bake in 350° oven for 20–25 minutes. Turn cake out immediately onto a linen towel which has been dampened with hot water. Strip wax paper off immediately. Trim crusty edges. Roll cake and towel together lengthwise and place in refrigerator to cool. Take out, unroll, spread with whipped cream which has been flavored with 2 tablespoons of powdered sugar, vanilla, or cognac and a tiny pinch of salt. Reroll carefully. Refrigerate. Serve sliced and topped with chocolate sauce or sprinkle entire roll with sifted powdered sugar.

CHOCOLATE SAUCE:

2 squares unsweetened chocolate	Dash of salt
6 tablespoons light cream	3 tablespoons butter
½ cup sugar	1 teaspoon vanilla

Melt chocolate in cream over low heat. Add sugar and salt. Take off heat; add butter and vanilla. Stir constantly until cooled. Makes 1 cup sauce.

CHOCOLATE RUM SOUFFLÉ

12 almond macaroons (whole)	6 eggs, separated
½ cup rum or cognac	24 ladyfingers
16 ounces semi-sweet	½ pint whipping cream, whipped
chocolate	Grated chocolate, optional
6 tablespoons water	garnish
7 tablespoons sugar	

Soak macaroons in rum or cognac. Melt chocolate in double boiler with water and 6 tablespoons sugar. Mix well, remove from stove and add egg yolks one at a time. Let mixture cool. Beat egg whites, adding 1 tablespoon sugar to make them stiff. Carefully fold egg whites into chocolate mixture. Line the bottom and sides of an 8" spring-form pan with split ladyfingers. Add half the chocolate mixture and then a layer of soaked macaroons. Add remaining chocolate mixture, top with ladyfingers and refrigerate overnight. To serve, unmold, top with whipped cream and sprinkle on grated chocolate.

FLOATING ISLAND WITH STRAWBERRIES

CUSTARD:

1½ cups milk	2 teaspoons cornstarch
7 egg yolks	1 teaspoon vanilla extract
1½ cups sugar	1 teaspoon lemon rind

Scald milk. In a mixing bowl beat egg yolks until very pale yellow; gradually add sugar, stirring constantly until it forms a ribbon. Add cornstarch; blend in well. Pour mixture into top of double boiler, being sure water does not touch bottom of pan. Place over medium heat, and gradually add scalded milk, stirring constantly, cooking until mixture heavily coats spoon, approximately 25–30 minutes. Cool and refrigerate. When cool blend in vanilla and lemon rind. May be made a day ahead.

ISLANDS:

    4 egg whites   *¼ cup fine sugar*
    ⅛ teaspoon cream of tartar   *Milk (approximately 2 cups)*

Beat egg whites with cream of tartar until they form stiff peaks. Gradually add sugar, stirring constantly. In a large skillet pour milk to a depth of 1½". Bring milk to a simmer; do not boil. When simmering, spoon in egg-size heaps of egg whites and let cook 2–3 minutes. Turn, using 2 utensils for control. Cook an additional 2 minutes. Remove with a slotted spoon and drain on wax paper. May be made several hours before serving.

FRUIT AND DECORATION:

    1 pint whole strawberries or   *3 ounces slivered almonds,*
      raspberries, washed and capped   *toasted*

Using a deep clear serving bowl begin layering with egg white puffs, then some strawberries, and coat with custard. Repeat, ending with custard on top. Reserve a few strawberries to decorate with. Before serving, sprinkle with almonds.

FRENCH CHOCOLATE SILK PIE

CRUST:

    1¼ cups crumbled vanilla wafers
    1½ tablespoons sugar
    6 tablespoons butter, melted

Combine above ingredients and line the edge and bottom of a 9" pie plate. Bake 7 minutes in 350° oven, then cool.

FILLING:

1½ sticks butter, room
   temperature
1 cup and 2 tablespoons superfine
   sugar
1½ squares unsweetened chocolate,
   melted

1½ teaspoons vanilla
3 eggs
½ pint whipping cream
¼ cup sliced almonds, toasted

Beat butter until creamy. Add sugar a little at a time. Continue beating, then add melted chocolate and vanilla. Add 2 eggs and beat 3 minutes. Add remaining egg and beat 3 minutes. Pour mixture into cool pie shell and refrigerate. Serve topped with whipped cream and almonds.

FRESH FRUIT ICE CREAM

4 eggs, beaten
2 cups sugar
5 cups puréed fresh fruit*
4 cups whipping cream
1 teaspoon vanilla

½ teaspoon salt
Ice cream salt
Crushed ice
Ice cream freezer (gallon size)

Add sugar to beaten eggs. Then add fruit, cream, vanilla, and salt; mix thoroughly. Pour in freezer. Pack freezer with ice and ice cream salt according to freezer directions. Makes about 3 quarts.

* Some suggestions are: strawberries, figs, peaches, or oranges.

LACE COOKIES

2 cups old-fashioned rolled oats
1 tablespoon flour
2 cups white sugar
½ teaspoon salt

2 sticks melted butter
2 eggs, beaten
1 teaspoon vanilla

Put the oats, flour, sugar, and salt into a large bowl and mix well. Pour very hot butter over the mixture and stir until the sugar has melted. Add eggs and vanilla; stir well. Preheat oven to 325°. Cover cookie sheets with ungreased aluminum foil. Drop ½ level teaspoon of the mixture on foil, 2 inches apart. Cooking time is about 10–12 minutes. Watch carefully. When cookies are completely cooled, foil will peel off. Store in airtight containers. Makes about 6 dozen.

MOCHA MERINGUE

4 egg whites
½ teaspoon cream of tartar
¼ teaspoon salt
1 cup sugar
1 teaspoon vanilla

4 cups coffee ice cream,
  softened*
½ cup sliced almonds, toasted
½ cup chocolate sauce (see index)

Beat egg whites, cream of tartar, and salt until frothy. Gradually add sugar, beating constantly until stiff. Add vanilla and beat one minute. On brown paper, drop 9 meringue kisses. Grease a 9″ pie plate with butter. With remaining meringue, form shell in the pie plate and cook in 300° oven for 50 to 60 minutes. Be sure meringue is thoroughly dry. Cook kisses at same time, approximately 25 minutes, and watch until kisses are nicely browned. After cooked and completely cooled, fill pie shell by layering with 2 cups ice cream, ¼ cup almonds and ¼ cup sauce. Repeat for second layer. Place 8 kisses around top and 1 in center. Trickle remaining chocolate over the top. Place in freezer.

* Another flavor ice cream may be substituted.

MOUSSE À LEMON

8 eggs, separated
1 cup sugar
3 grated lemon rinds
½ cup lemon juice
2 tablespoons gelatin
½ cup cold water

2 dozen ladyfingers
½ pint whipping cream
2 teaspoons powdered sugar
¼ teaspoon vanilla
Decoration: grated lemon rind,
  fresh mint sprigs

In top of a double boiler, not over heat, beat egg yolks until thick and very pale yellow. Add sugar gradually while beating constantly. Stir in lemon rinds and lemon juice. Place over gently boiling water, being sure water does not touch bottom of double boiler. Cook, stirring constantly, until sauce gets hot and is a thick custard. Soften gelatin in cold water and add to hot lemon mixture, stirring well until gelatin is dissolved. Pour mixture into a bowl and let cool throughly, stirring occasionally before folding in stiffly beaten egg whites.

Line 9" spring-form mold, sides and bottom with ladyfingers. Beat egg whites until stiff and fold into cooled lemon mixture. Pour into lined mold and refrigerate. Whip cream, adding powdered sugar and vanilla. Top lemon mixture with whipped cream. Decorate with grated lemon rind and fresh mint leaves.

ORANGE CRÈME BRULÉE

1 pint whipping cream
1 pint light cream
8 egg yolks
½ cup (packed) dark brown sugar

¼ teaspoon salt
1 tablespoon orange extract†
¾ cup light brown sugar, sifted

Scald cream. Beat egg yolks, sugar, and salt until blended. Pour hot cream very slowly into egg mixture while beating with wire whisk. Add orange extract. Pour into a 2-quart rectangular baking dish. Place in a pan and add hot water to a depth of 1". Bake in 300° oven until a silver knife comes out clean—approximately 1 hour. When cool, refrigerate until mixture is set. Cover top of custard with ¼" sifted light brown sugar. Place custard in a pan of ice and put under broiler flame to caramelize sugar—approximately 2 minutes. This may be prepared in advance, but caramelize the sugar right before serving.

† Vanilla extract may be substituted.

PECAN CRISPS

1 teaspoon soda
3½ cups flour
1 cup white sugar
1 cup brown sugar
1½ sticks softened butter

2 eggs, lightly beaten
1 teaspoon vanilla
½ teaspoon salt
1 cup chopped pecans

Sift soda and flour together. In a bowl cream white and brown sugar with butter. Fold in eggs, vanilla, salt, flour, soda, and nuts. Form two rolls 2½ inches in diameter; chill in refrigerator for 12 hours. Bake thinly sliced cookies in 350° oven for about ten minutes. Watch carefully. Makes approximately 8 dozen.

PECAN PIE

2 eggs
½ cup sugar
½ cup dark Karo syrup
2 tablespoons soft butter
1 cup chopped pecans
1 teaspoon vanilla

8" uncooked pie crust
Whole pecans for decorating
1 cup heavy cream, whipped
(optional)
1 ounce semi-sweet chocolate
(optional)

Beat eggs and add sugar, Karo syrup, butter, chopped pecans and vanilla. Mix well. Put mixture into uncooked 8" pie crust, decorate with whole pecans, and bake in 375° oven for 30–35 minutes. Can be baked day before. Serve hot or cold with whipped cream or brush on thin layer of melted semi-sweet chocolate.

PRALINES

2½ cups sugar
1 cup half-and-half cream

1 tablespoon butter
2 cups pecan halves

In a heavy iron pan, combine 2 cups sugar with cream and butter and bring to a boil. In a separate heavy saucepan, melt ½ cup sugar until it is caramel color. Add the cream, butter, and sugar mixture to the caramel mixture. Add pecans and cook to the soft-ball stage (235° on candy thermometer). Remove from heat and beat until it thickens. Drop onto wax paper to harden. Yields 2 dozen pralines 2½ to 3 inches in diameter.

STRAWBERRY SHORTCAKE

2 cups sifted flour
½ cup light brown sugar
1 cup butter
1 cup whipping cream

2 tablespoons powdered sugar
2 pints strawberries, hulled and
washed

Mix flour and brown sugar and work in butter. Place on floured board and pat to ½″ thickness. Do not roll. Cut into desired shapes, squares or circles, and bake in a 325° oven on a cookie sheet for 20 to 25 minutes. Whip cream, sweetening with powdered sugar. Place strawberries over shortcake and top with whipped cream. Yields 1 dozen shortcakes.

TARTE AUX PÊCHES

9″ pie crust, uncooked
1 egg, separated (room temperature)
1½ pounds peaches
Juice of ½ lemon
¼ cup white sugar
¼ cup brown sugar

1 teaspoon cinnamon
Pinch ground nutmeg
Pinch ground cloves
Pinch salt
2 tablespoons butter
¼ cup whipping cream

Brush inside of pie crust with unbeaten egg white. Peel peaches; cut in half and pit. Arrange halves in an overlapping pattern around bottom of pie crust. Squeeze lemon juice over the fruit. Combine both sugars, cinnamon, nutmeg, cloves, and salt, and sprinkle over fruit. Place dots of butter over peaches and bake in 350° oven for 25 minutes. Remove. Heat cream to lukewarm; stir in egg yolk with a whisk. Pour cream mixture carefully over the fruit. Return to 350° oven for 15–20 minutes, or until the top is brown and the custard is set in center. Serve at room temperature.

BANANA NUT BREAD

½ cup shortening
½ cup butter
3 cups sugar
2 teaspoons vanilla
4 eggs
¼ teaspoon salt

3½ cups flour
2 teaspoons soda
½ cup buttermilk or ½ cup milk with ½ teaspoon vinegar added
6 small bananas, mashed
1 cup chopped pecans

Cream shortening, butter, sugar, and vanilla until fluffy. Add eggs, one at a time, blending thoroughly after each addition. In a separate bowl sift salt, flour, and soda twice. Add dry ingredients alternately with milk to the creamy mixture. Combine bananas and nuts and blend into mixture. Pour into a greased angel-food cake pan and cook in 350° oven for 1½ to 1¾ hours. Use a cake tester. If preferred this may be cooked in 2 greased loaf pans (9⅝ x 5½ x 2¾″) for 1 hour and 10 minutes.

WINE JELLY WITH FRUIT AND SAUCE

2 envelopes unflavored gelatin	Juice of 1 lemon
1 cup water	2½ cups wine (½ sherry, ½ port)
½ cup sugar	

Soften gelatin in ¼ cup cold water. In a saucepan heat sugar in ¾ cup water until sugar dissolves; add softened gelatin and stir until dissolved. Remove from fire; stir in lemon juice and wine. Pour into a lightly-greased 1-quart ring mold and chill at least 4 hours. May be made the day before serving.

SAUCE:

2 cups milk	1 teaspoon vanilla
3 egg yolks	½ pint whipping cream, whipped
½ cup sugar	

Scald milk. In a mixing bowl beat egg yolks until very pale yellow; gradually add sugar, stirring constantly until it forms a ribbon. Pour mixture into top of double boiler, being sure water does not touch bottom of pan. Place over medium heat, and gradually add scalded milk, stirring constantly; cooking until mixture heavily coats spoon, approximately 25–30 minutes. Cool. Refrigerate. Sauce may be made a day ahead to this point. Blend vanilla and whipped cream into cold mixture several hours before serving. Refrigerate sauce until ready to serve.

FRUIT:

Apple slices	Pear slices
Orange sections	Seedless grapes
Strawberries	

Unmold jelly onto serving dish; surround and fill center with selected fruit. Spoon some sauce over jelly and fruit; serve remaining sauce in a sauceboat.

BISCUITS

2 cups unsifted flour   4 tablespoons shortening
1 teaspoon salt   ½ teaspoon soda
5 teaspoons baking powder   1 cup buttermilk

Sift flour with salt and baking powder. Cut in shortening. Combine soda and buttermilk and add to the dry ingredients. Handle lightly. Roll dough ½″ thick and cut into 2″ rounds. Bake on ungreased sheet in 450° oven for about 10 to 12 minutes. Yield 24 biscuits.

CALAS TOUT CHAUD

1 teaspoon dry yeast   ¼ cup sugar
½ cup warm water   ½ teaspoon salt
1½ cups cooked rice, cooled to ⅛ teaspoon nutmeg
    lukewarm   Deep hot fat
3 eggs, well beaten   Powdered sugar
1 cup sifted flour

Soften yeast in warm water and stir in lukewarm rice, mixing well. Cover and let rise several hours or overnight. Add eggs, flour, sugar, salt, and nutmeg. Beat well and let stand in warm place 20–30 minutes. Drop by tablespoon into hot fat and fry until golden brown. Serve sprinkled with powdered sugar.

COFFEE CAKE

DOUGH:

1 cup milk   1 tablespoon grated lemon peel
1½ sticks butter   5 tablespoons sugar
2 packages dry yeast   2 egg yolks, room temperature
⅛ teaspoon sugar   2 whole eggs, room temperature
4⅓ cups flour   1 teaspoon salt

Scald milk and let cool to lukewarm. Melt butter and let cool. Dissolve yeast in lukewarm milk and add ⅛ teaspoon sugar. In a large, dry, and warm bowl, mix yeast with ⅓ cup flour, stirring until smooth. Sprinkle some flour on top and let rise ½ hour. Add lemon peel, sugar, egg yolks, whole eggs, salt, and cooled butter. Stir in remaining flour ½ cup at a time, and beat until smooth. Cover and let rise in a warm, draft-free place, for 1½ hours or until double in bulk. Meanwhile, prepare filling. When dough has doubled, turn onto floured surface, as dough is ready for filling.

NUT FILLING:

1 cup sugar
¾ cup water
1 lemon peel, grated

10 ounces ground pecans or
  walnuts
1 recipe coffee-cake dough
1 beaten egg

Slowly boil sugar and water for 10 minutes. Add lemon peel and nuts and cook until brown, about 5 minutes. If too thick, a little milk may be added. Let cool.

Roll out dough on floured surface to form a rectangle ¼" thick. Spread cooled filling over dough. Roll up jelly-roll fashion, making roll long. Arrange (curve to fit) on a greased baking pan, seam down, and brush dough with beaten egg. Let rise 45 minutes. Brush again with egg, prick top, and bake in 350° oven for 45 minutes or until golden brown. This will stay moist several days after baking. If preferred, you may form two smaller logs instead of one large one.

CREAM CHEESE FILLING:

¼ stick butter, softened
8 ounces cream cheese
⅓ cup sugar
1 large egg

½ teaspoon grated lemon peel
½ teaspoon vanilla
⅓ recipe coffee-cake dough
1 beaten egg

Cream softened butter. Add cream cheese and beat until fluffy. Add sugar and continue beating. Add 1 egg, lemon peel, vanilla, and beat again. Roll out a round of dough the size of a pie pan (about ½" thick). Reserve some dough to make a lattice top. Place in a greased pie pan and add filling. Cut strips of dough and form lattice top. Let rise 45 minutes. Brush top with beaten egg and bake in 350° oven for 30 minutes, or until golden brown. Serve warm.

APPLE FILLING:

⅓ recipe coffee-cake dough
1½ cups sliced, peeled apples
2 tablespoons sugar

½ teaspoon cinnamon
½ stick butter, melted and cooled
1 beaten egg

Roll out a circle of dough the size of a pie pan (½" thick) saving some dough to make a lattice top. Place dough in a greased pie pan. Arrange sliced apples over dough and sprinkle with sugar and cinnamon. Distribute melted butter over all. Cut strips of dough and form lattice top. Let rise 45 minutes. Brush dough with beaten egg and bake in 350° oven for 30 minutes, or until golden brown.

CORNBREAD

½ cup flour
1 cup white corn meal
1 teaspoon baking powder
½ teaspoon soda
1 teaspoon salt
2 tablespoons sugar

1 cup buttermilk
1 egg
2 tablespoons shortening (melted)
1 medium jalapeno pepper, chopped
　　finely (optional)

Put flour, meal, baking powder, soda, salt, and sugar into sifter; sift altogether into bowl. Add milk and stir well. Add egg and shortening and beat well. Add jalapeno pepper to batter if desired. Can be prepared to this point several hours ahead. When ready to bake; stir, pour into hot greased 9" iron skillet or cornbread-stick pan. Place in preheated 400° oven for approximately 20 minutes or until brown.

CRÊPES

2 cups flour
3 cups milk
2 eggs

1 teaspoon salt
1 tablespoon melted butter
½ stick butter, clarified

Sift flour into mixing bowl and gradually add milk, beating with a wire whisk. Add eggs, salt, and 1 tablespoon butter. Beat until fluffy, and let stand for 20 minutes to allow flour to absorb liquids. This prevents tearing when turning crêpes. Beat again before ready to use. Pour 2 teaspoons clarified butter into frying pan, coating bottom. Heat pan until almost smoking. Pour just enough crêpe batter into pan to make a thin coating. Lift pan and roll mixture until bottom is covered. Loosen edges with spatula and flip when brown. Brown other side and remove to platter. Continue until batter is used up. These can be stacked as cooked. Roll up with favorite preserve or syrup. Yields 16 (9″) crêpes. If a sweet crêpe is desired, add 1 tablespoon sugar to batter.

FRENCH MARKET DOUGHNUTS

1 package yeast
½ cup lukewarm water
1 egg beaten, room temperature
¼ cup sugar
1 teaspoon salt

1 cup canned evaporated milk,
    room temperature
3 cups flour, sifted
Vegetable oil
Powdered sugar

In a mixing bowl dissolve yeast in lukewarm water. Add egg, sugar, salt, and evaporated milk. Gradually blend in flour, mixing well. Cover bowl with moistened towel and place in refrigerator overnight. Turn dough onto a floured surface and roll out to ¼″ thickness. Cut into 2½″ squares and allow dough to dry on floured board, 10–12 minutes before frying. Fry in 1″ very hot vegetable oil, turning once, cooking until golden brown, approximately 3 minutes. With slotted spoon, remove doughnuts and place on a paper towel to drain. Sprinkle liberally with powdered sugar. Dough will keep in refrigerator for several days. Makes about 2–2½ dozen.

GINGERBREAD

3 eggs
1 cup sugar
1 cup molasses (unsulphured)
1 cup butter, room temperature
1 teaspoon powdered ginger
1 teaspoon powdered cinnamon

1 teaspoon powdered cloves
⅛ teaspoon salt
2 teaspoons soda, soaked in ⅛ cup
    of hot water
2 cups flour
1 cup boiling water

Combine eggs, sugar, molasses, butter, ginger, cinnamon, cloves, and salt in a bowl and beat well. Add dissolved soda. Sift in flour and beat well. Add boiling water, beat lightly and quickly. Pour this thin batter into two 8″ square greased pans immediately, and bake in 350° oven for 45 minutes. Serve plain or top with warm lemon sauce.

OLD-FASHIONED PUMPKIN BREAD

1⅔ cups flour
¼ teaspoon baking powder
1 teaspoon soda
¾ teaspoon salt
½ teaspoon cinnamon
½ teaspoon nutmeg
⅓ cup shortening

1⅓ cups sugar
½ teaspoon vanilla
2 eggs
1 cup cooked pumpkin
⅓ cup water
½ cup pecans, chopped

Grease a 9⅝ x 5½ x 2¾″ loaf pan. Sift together flour, baking powder, soda, salt, cinnamon, and nutmeg. Cream shortening, sugar, and vanilla. Then add eggs, one at a time, beating thoroughly after each addition. Stir in pumpkin. Stir in dry ingredients in 4 additions, alternating with water until just smooth. Add chopped nuts and pour into loaf pan. Bake in 350° oven for 40–45 minutes. Use a cake tester. Turn out on rack and cool right side up. Serve at room temperature. This is good with softened cream cheese.

ORANGE MUFFINS

2½ cups flour
2 teaspoons baking powder
½ teaspoon salt
1½ sticks butter, softened
1⅔ cups sugar

3 eggs, beaten
1 teaspoon vanilla
½ cup orange juice
Grated rind of 2 oranges
Powdered sugar for garnish

Sift flour, baking powder, and salt. In a separate bowl, cream butter and sugar; add eggs, vanilla, orange juice and rind. Combine liquid and dry ingredients and stir lightly until batter is moist but still lumpy. Use non-stick muffin pans or grease small 1¾″ muffin pans with oil and dust with flour. Half fill muffin pans and bake 15 minutes in a 350° oven. Remove from oven and top with powdered sugar. Makes 3 dozen.

INDEX

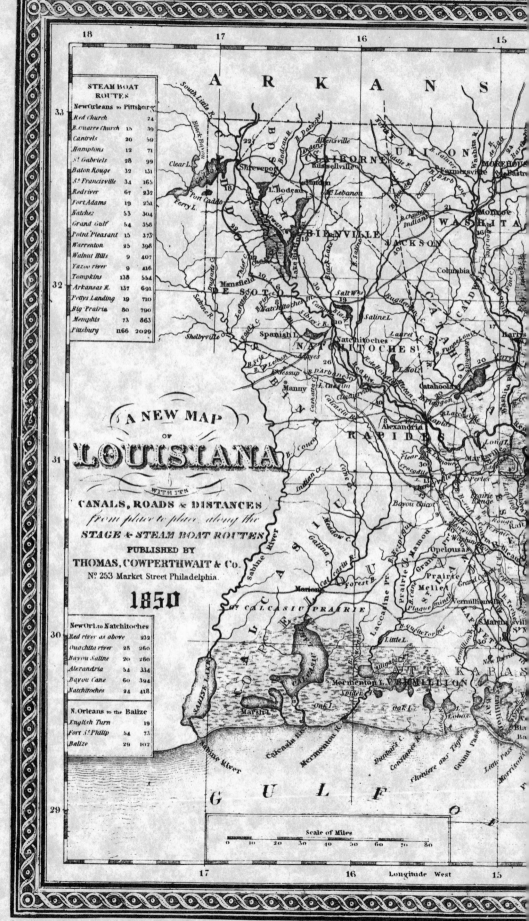

A NEW MAP OF LOUISIANA

WITH ITS

CANALS, ROADS & DISTANCES

from place to place along the

STAGE & STEAM BOAT ROUTES

PUBLISHED BY

THOMAS, COWPERTHWAIT & Co.

Nº 253 Market Street Philadelphia.

1850

STEAM BOAT ROUTES

New Orleans to Pittsburg

Red Church		24
B. Ouarre Church	15	39
Cantrels	20	59
Hamptons	12	71
St Gabriels	28	99
Baton Rouge	32	131
St Francisville	34	165
Redriver	67	232
Fort Adams	19	251
Natchez	53	304
Grand Gulf	54	358
Point Pleasant	15	373
Warrenton	25	398
Walnut Hills	9	407
Yazoo river	9	416
Tompkins	138	554
Arkansas R.	137	691
Pettys Landing	19	710
Big Prairie	80	790
Memphis	73	863
Pittsburg	n66	2029

New Orl. to Natchitoches

Red river as above		232
Ouachita river	28	260
Bayou Saline	20	280
Alexandria	54	334
Bayou Cane	60	394
Natchitoches	24	418

N. Orleans to the Balize

English Turn		19
Fort St Philip	54	73
Balize	29	102

Scale of Miles

0 10 20 30 40 50 60 70 80